"The content and style of this excellent book h
cantly improve the well-being and quality of l
autism and their families. I endorse the theoret
siastically use and recommend the activities with adolescents and to my colleagues."

—**Tony Attwood**, author of *The Complete Guide to Asperger's Syndrome*

"As the incidence of autism has risen to 1 in 66, becoming aware of autism is evolving to accepting autism as part of the human family. The challenges of the autism spectrum can be gritty and unwelcome, so changing the changeable and finding a peaceful balance is vital. The mindfulness-based activities skillfully applied by McHenry and Moog can help teens and their supporters to calm their minds and bodies, have fun, and enjoy their lives—*with practice*."

—**Robert A. Naseef, PhD**, in private practice at Alternative Choices and author of *Autism in the Family: Caring and Coping Together*

"With their *Autism Playbook for Teens*, Irene McHenry and Carol Moog offer a manual for well-being for youths—not only for young people on the autism spectrum, but for others as well. The authors' experience and their understanding of adolescents on the spectrum are clearly evident from cover to cover. Written in an authentic, accessible, and sensitive way, this book radiates understanding of the struggles teens on the spectrum face every day. It provides practical yet imaginative exercises for managing emotions, relating to others, and achieving independence based on the foundation of mindfulness. The fact that this book directly addresses the teenage reader is a unique and enormously helpful feature, but it can also be very useful to parents and others who are part of the young person's world. This is the playbook many youths have needed for a long time."

—**Trish Broderick, PhD**, research associate, Bennett Pierce Prevention Research Center, Pennsylvania State University, University Park, PA

"You may have heard phrases such as 'the miracle of mindfulness' or 'the mindfulness revolution.' What's all the hoopla about? Well, it turns out that attentional skills can be dramatically improved through systematic exercise, and mindfulness seems to provide the most effective way of doing that.

The specific focus skills that mindfulness develops are precisely those needed by people on the autism spectrum: the ability to concentrate; the ability to detect cues from the environment; and the ability to experience emotional sensations with a kind of gentle matter-of-factness, not suppressing them, but also not holding onto them. These skills working together can help people experience more connectedness, pick up on social cues, and manage their emotional bodies. The book you have in your hand represents a practical guide for achieving these deep goals."

—**Shinzen Young, PhD**

"Grounded in creative mindfulness practices and Irene McHenry and Carol Moog's deep understanding of the challenges faced by teens on the autism spectrum, this inspired autism playbook offers invaluable support to teens, their parents, and helping professionals."

—**Richard Brady, MS**, president and cofounder of the Mindfulness in Education Network and co-editor with Irene McHenry of *Tuning In: Mindfulness in Teaching and Learning*

"*The Autism Playbook for Teens* is an invaluable resource for adolescents that will support their emotional and social health. Through the stories in each chapter, teens will realize that they are not alone in their struggles. Using the clear and simple instructions for the practical exercises offered, teens will be able to experience greater calm and connection to themselves and others. This is an extraordinary book. Let the play begin."

—**Diane Reibel, PhD**, director of the Mindfulness Institute at the Jefferson Myrna-Brind Center of Integrative Medicine and coauthor of *Teaching Mindfulness: A Practical Guide for Clinicians and Educators*

the *instant help* solutions series

Young people today need mental health resources more than ever. That's why New Harbinger created the **Instant Help Solutions Series** especially for teens. Written by leading psychologists, these evidence-based self-help books offer practical tips and strategies for dealing with a variety of mental health issues and life challenges teens face, such as depression, anxiety, bullying, eating disorders, trauma, and self-esteem problems.

Studies have shown that young people who learn healthy coping skills early on are better able to navigate problems later in life. Engaging and easy-to-use, these books provide teens with the tools they need to thrive—at home, at school, and on into adulthood.

This series is part of the **New Harbinger Instant Help Books** imprint, founded by renowned child psychologist Lawrence Shapiro. For a complete list of books in this series, visit newharbinger.com.

the **autism playbook** for **teens**

imagination-based mindfulness activities to **calm yourself, build independence** & **connect with others**

IRENE McHENRY, PhD
CAROL MOOG, PhD

Instant Help Books
An Imprint of New Harbinger Publications, Inc.

Publisher's Note

Distributed in Canada by Raincoast Books

Instant Help Books
An Imprint of New Harbinger Publications, Inc.
5674 Shattuck Avenue
Oakland, CA 94609
www.newharbinger.com

Cover design by Amy Shoup
Edited by Will DeRooy
Acquired by Wendy Millstine

Library of Congress Cataloging-in-Publication Data

McHenry, Irene.
The autism playbook for teens : imagination-based mindfulness activities to calm yourself, build independence, and connect with others / Irene McHenry, Carol Moog ; foreword by Susan Kaiser Greenland.
pages cm. -- (The instant help solutions series)
Summary: "Teens with autism are natural observers--able to study, imitate, and learn social behavior. The Autism Playbook for Teens is designed to empower these strengths with mindfulness strategies and scripts, while also helping teens reduce anxiety, manage emotions, be more aware in the present moment, and connect with others. This book offers a unique, strengths-based approach to help teens with autism and Asperger's develop social skills , strengthen communication, and thrive"-- Provided by publisher.
ISBN 978-1-62625-009-3 (paperback : acid-free paper) -- ISBN 978-1-62625-010-9 (pdf e-book) -- ISBN 978-1-62625-011-6 (epub) 1. Autism spectrum disorders. 2. Social interaction in adolescence. I. Moog, Carol. II. Title.
RC553.A88M386 2014
616.85'88200835--dc23

2014006468

Printed in the United States of America

16 15 14

10 9 8 7 6 5 4 3 2 1 First Printing

For Ari Trey Masters, Irene's gifted, clever, and loving godson, who provided invaluable feedback on drafts of this book; and for Jessie Pries, Carol's ever curious, ninety-four-year-old mother.

contents

foreword v

acknowledgments ix

Part I
Calm Your Body and Mind

Chapter 1 Just Breathe: Focus and Calm Yourself 3

Chapter 2 Soar with Your Butterflies: Calm Your Anxiety 11

Chapter 3 Create a Pause Button: Get Comfortable 17

Chapter 4 Light the Stage: Choose the Best Focus 23

Chapter 5 Groove with Gravity: Feel Solid in Your Body 29

Part II
Use Your Thoughts and Feelings to Build Your Independence

Chapter 6 Your Body Is the Actor: Identify Your Feelings 37

Chapter 7 The Astonishing Energy of Feelings: Use Your Feelings as Power 45

Chapter 8 Basic Meltdown Prevention: Managing Anger 51

Chapter 9 Your Mind Is the Stage: Get Flexible and Switch Roles 65

Chapter 10 Makeover Magic: Improve Your Self-Esteem 77

Part III

Reach Out to Connect with Others and Direct Your Life

Chapter 11	Play the Role of a Scientist: Get Curious	89
Chapter 12	You Are the Director: Advocate for Yourself	99
Chapter 13	The Positive Channel: Build Your Health and Happiness	105
Chapter 14	Practice Kindness: Make Friends	113
Chapter 15	Design Your Own Stage: Prepare for Your Scenes	125
Chapter 16	Live Your Own Scripts: Direct Your Next Steps	133

foreword

The teenage years are difficult to navigate, and mine were no exception. Back then I could have used some help, but if someone had given me a book about mindfulness I probably would have rolled my eyes. Life was hard enough, and I likely would have bridled against any well-meaning adult who I thought was trying to fix something "wrong" with me. Looking back, I wish I had known a couple of things about mindfulness when I was a teenager, because it has made my adult life much easier.

The authors of this book describe mindfulness as "a way to become more aware of what you're thinking and feeling so that you can calm yourself, focus, and connect better with yourself and others." That's a good description of how mindfulness initially helped me. But, as the years have passed, mindfulness has come to mean much more. Mindfulness has become a way of life. I don't want to give you the impression that I'm mindful all the time, because I'm not. But mindfulness-based calming strategies allow me to see what's happening in and around me more clearly, and a mindful worldview reminds me that I can choose to look at life differently than many of my peers. This shift in perspective has made an enormous difference in how I feel and how I respond to challenging situations.

Let me share three aspects of a mindful worldview that have helped me and the children and teens that I've taught for over a decade. The first is that actions have consequences. When I was a teenager, plenty of adults told me this, and I thought I knew what they meant. But it turns out that I only understood half of the equation. I was a perfectionist, so it made sense that I interpreted the phrase "actions have consequences" to mean that if things didn't go right I had done something wrong. I was already pretty hard on myself, so this sage piece of advice turned out to be just another way to beat myself up. I wish I had understood earlier that what's happening now is the result of causes and conditions that have happened before. Some of what has already happened was in our control, but here's the point: much of what has already happened was completely outside of our control. There's absolutely nothing we can do about what's outside of our control, but there's a whole lot we can do about what's in our control. As a teenager, I knew intuitively that my actions were my own. For instance, I understood that if I didn't study for a test and I bombed it, my bad grade was on me. What I didn't understand was that other people's actions were also their own. In other words, I didn't realize that if other kids talked behind my back or treated me badly, it would ultimately have a bigger negative impact on their lives than it would have on mine.

Thoughts have consequences too, and they tend to come before actions. That's the second aspect of a mindful worldview that I wish I had learned earlier on. All too often we believe that we're stuck with our thoughts. We see that they're getting in our way, but we don't believe that there's anything we can do about it. The good news is that's not the case. We can develop a different relationship to thoughts, and when we do, our lives tend to get a whole lot easier.

We know that thoughts lead to actions, and both have consequences. But there's more. The third aspect of a mindful worldview that I'd like to share has to do with what comes before thoughts. Often it's an idea or a worldview that has consequences too. Sometimes we're not aware of it, but the reason we do or say something is motivated by a specific idea. About a decade ago, I was teaching mindfulness to young children and there was a boy in the class who had a medical diagnosis and came to school with a shadow aide. He was uncomfortable sitting in the circle with the other children, so we encouraged him to sit with his shadow aide on a couch nearby. He was welcome to participate, but for the most part he didn't seem interested. Imagine our surprise when the school administrator got a call from the boy's doctor saying that, unbeknownst to us, she had been encouraging him to practice mindfulness-based calming strategies for quite a while but the boy had refused. Something had changed—at his recent appointment the boy taught the doctor a mindfulness activity he had learned in school. When the doctor asked why he had changed his mind, the boy said that he hadn't wanted to do the exercises before because he thought they were only for kids with problems. Now that everyone in his class was practicing mindfulness, he had decided to give it a try. For me, this is a profound example of how ideas have consequences. The consequence of my student's idea that mindfulness was only for kids with problems got in the way of his learning something new. When he realized his idea was incomplete—that mindfulness was for everybody—he was able to shift his perspective and take advantage of what mindfulness had to offer.

I hope you enjoy this book. It's the culmination of the authors' significant body of work sharing mindfulness with teens. I've been waiting a long time for a practical, wise book on the subject and am delighted that it's here. May it serve children, teens, and families everywhere.

—Susan Kaiser Greenland, JD
Writer, innovator, parent, mindfulness educator, co-founder of The Inner Kids Foundation, and author of *The Mindful Child*

acknowledgments

We wish to acknowledge our collegial writing partnership and great friendship that embodies the skills and values this book is designed to develop. Our hope is that readers will share the fun, experimentation, focused attention, and playful spirit that went into its creation.

We extend gratitude to the many students and learning communities that were instrumental in providing a foundation for our work. The international network of Friends schools drawn together by Friends Council on Education, the Miquon School, Delaware Valley Friends School, and the University of Pennsylvania (Social Skills Seminar) provided tangible working connections to children, teens, young adults, and the worlds of play, imagination, learning differences, and mindfulness in teaching and learning.

Our thanks to Abby Huntington, Eric Mitchell, Wendy Ross, Beulah Trey, and Sonia Voynow for their wise, invaluable collegial support, and thanks to New Harbinger editors Wendy Millstine and Jess Beebe for their guidance and supportive feedback throughout the writing of this book. We extend deep appreciation to our pioneering mindfulness teachers and clinical colleagues who inspired us: Jon Kabat-Zinn, Thich Nhat Hanh, Shinzen Young, Diane Reibel, Trish Broderick, Larry Ladden, Richard Brady, Polly Young-Eisendrath, and Susan Kaiser Greenland. And, we offer a very special thank-you to Temple Grandin for the gifts she has given all of us in understanding autism.

Finally, we appreciate the significant love and support from our families in bringing this work to fruition: Roger Moog for his generosity and humor, Randy Granger for his ingenuity and insight, Julie Holcomb and Michael McHenry Koehler for their limitless spontaneity and creativity, and the joyful, lively imaginations of our grandchildren—Henry, Brayden, Charles, and Stella.

Dear Teen Reader,

We know that as a teenager, you have to deal with many stressful situations every day. You probably feel overwhelmed and stressed much of the time—sometimes you feel up, sometimes you feel down, and sometimes you just feel stuck in a place you can't get out of. This book will show you how you can reduce stress, calm your nerves, work with frustration, and become better at relating to other people through *mindfulness.* Mindfulness has to do with becoming more aware of what you are thinking and feeling. Learning to use the tools of mindfulness will give you creative ways to calm yourself, focus, and connect better with yourself and others. It can help you recover after you suffer a meltdown or even prevent you from having one in the first place.

We have designed this book for you to use on your own, without needing to be part of a group or a class, to help you learn mindfulness skills by means of imaginative exercises. You can do most of these exercises in the safety and privacy of your own space, such as your bedroom. They are yours to use and customize as you wish; you can practice and play with them to explore different feelings and ways to act in various situations. Even though you can do them on your own, you can also choose to do some or all of them with someone else, such as a friend, a family member, or someone who knows about mindfulness. Most of the exercises probably involve trying something you have never done before, and that might be challenging. We encourage you to just take a deep breath, feel the challenge, and try these new things anyway. By practicing each exercise, you will gain confidence, increase your flexibility, and be able to have more fun with yourself and others.

You may notice that many of the exercises are drawn from the world of acting and theater. Acting exercises can help people with autism learn and practice using knowledge of how people's bodies and faces show their feelings, how people's tones of voice change in different roles, and how different scripts work in different situations to sharpen their relationship skills.

Part I of this book is about calming your body and mind. Part II teaches you to use your thoughts and feelings in ways that will help you become more independent. Part III is about reaching out to connect with others. If you work through the parts and chapters in order, and build your skills by practicing the exercises, by the end of this book you will be able to go out and start creating the kinds of relationships you want to have.

We wish to assure you, however, that you don't have to change who you are to use this book. Being a teen on the autism spectrum, you are a unique, creative, energetic person. As you try out the exercises, just be yourself and see how they work. They are meant to build on the strengths of your creativity and imagination, and, when you put them into practice, you may discover you have even more strengths than you thought. We invite you to bring your curiosity, courage, and imagination as you experiment with being mindful.

Enjoy!

Carol and Irene

Dear Parents, Teachers, Counselors, and Other Professionals,

We are two licensed psychologists with over forty years of experience between us in the fields of autism and mindfulness. Given our many years of connection and our mutual respect for each other's work, we decided to team up to offer mindfulness tools with imagination-based exercises specifically for teens with autism.

The need for such a book has never been greater. The Centers for Disease Control (CDC) estimates that one in every sixty-eight children in the United States has been diagnosed with autism spectrum disorder (ASD), the highest prevalence since the CDC started tracking it in 2000, at which time the estimate was one in one hundred fifty. Parents and professionals are concerned with this dramatic increase.

This book uses mindfulness to develop skills that will help teens with autism live a fuller and more engaged life. It does so through appealingly playful exercises tailored to help teenagers reduce stress and anxiety, recover from meltdowns, constructively channel their emotional energies, and reach out to connect with others in positive ways. The exercises, designed to be practiced in various ways in a variety of settings, take into account the unique perspectives, sensory issues, neurological strengths, and challenges that teens with autism bring to their encounters with the social world. We seek to facilitate authentic engagement and awareness, leading to social interactions that are rewarding, interesting, and fun. Each exercise encourages a creative, playful approach but is grounded in well-documented clinical observations and recent empirical studies. Their design takes into account the real neurological differences of this special population and the unique approach needed to connect with and inspire these exceptional and fabulous teenagers.

This book is intended especially for teens on the autism spectrum who have some verbal language capacity (expressive and receptive language skills) and will be of value for parents, teachers, and other professionals who work with children, teenagers, and young adults on the autism spectrum.

Although this book is designed for teens to be able to use by themselves, parents and caregivers of teens on level 1 of the autism spectrum (*DSM-5*) may want to partner with teens to use this book as a resource. They can easily help teens practice the mindfulness exercises at home and adapt them to their own family context. Teachers, therapists, coaches, and counselors can use this book to work with teens individually or in groups, in educational and/or therapeutic contexts.

This book is structured so that readers will build skills sequentially, so please advise your teen to go through the chapters in order. The exercises are designed for teenagers to do on their own, and we recommend that you give your teen the freedom to practice in the comfort of his or her own private space, at his or her own pace.

The book is organized in three parts. Part I is about calming the body and mind. The exercises in these chapters build an essential foundation for the mindfulness skills that will be taught in the remainder of the book. Part II contains specific exercises related to noticing thoughts and feelings and using thoughts and feelings in positive ways. This is important for building independence and preparing for the work in part III, which is about reaching out to connect with others.

We hope you enjoy this book. Feel free to make creative adaptations as you wish.

Warmly,

Irene and Carol

Part I

Calm Your Body and Mind

Chapter 1

just breathe: focus and calm yourself

Usually, as soon as he gets up to go to school, Daniel starts to become nervous. Even if he has slept well, didn't have any nightmares, has finished all his homework, and doesn't have any tests that day, he starts to feel panicky and a little bit sick. He can hardly catch his breath. He can't understand why he feels this way. It just seems to be something he is stuck with. He hates feeling like this, which makes it even worse. His mother tells him to relax, but he can't.

Most days, Daniel stays in bed until his mother has given him several warnings and then starts yelling at him to get up. This makes him feel even more nervous. By the time he comes out of his room, he doesn't even feel like eating breakfast. This makes his mother even more upset.

Daniel just can't figure out how to start the school day without this terrible feeling. He wishes he had a way to calm himself when he wakes up feeling nervous.

Like Daniel, you may find that you have a lot of difficulty calming down when you feel nervous or stressed out. You might not know where this feeling is coming from or why it is happening. You might feel anxious or nervous often, even when there is nothing going on that is bothering you. If so, you aren't alone. Many teens with autism (and many teens without autism) are sometimes unexplainably nervous. But you can do something about it: you can learn how to calm yourself.

The amazing thing about calming yourself is that it only takes less than a minute. And you don't need anything special. All you have to do is use something that you have with you at all times: your breath!

That's right—you can develop a simple skill for calming yourself during times of stress by using your breath. The exercises in this chapter will help you develop your relaxation skills so that you can calm down when you need or want to, by just breathing naturally and focusing your attention on your breathing.

At first, it may feel odd to practice breathing, since you have been breathing your whole life. What is different in this case is that you are using your breathing on purpose, as a way to calm yourself.

The first exercise is a simple way to get to know your breath, get comfortable with your breathing, notice changes in your breathing, and feel at ease with your breathing from one moment to the next.

You can practice this exercise while sitting down or standing up. As with most of the exercises in this book, we recommend you try it first in a quiet place, without distractions. Once you get into the rhythm of your breathing, you can try doing this exercise while you are walking around.

Noticing is one of the most powerful tools you have for gathering information and learning about what's going on inside you as well as around you. You will have the opportunity to practice "noticing" in nearly all the exercises in this book. When you "notice" something, you just observe it—just become aware that it is there.

Exercise 1.1: Breathing In and Out with Ease

(Note: If it is comfortable for you, try this and the other breathing exercises in this book with your eyes closed. You can also choose to keep your eyes open, if that works better for you.)

Notice how your body is breathing right now. Don't try to change the way you are breathing right now in any way; just breathe naturally. You probably don't normally think of your body (and not you) as doing the breathing, but try noticing—observing—how your whole body is breathing in this moment. You might not realize it right now, but each breath is different from the breath that came before it. Try to notice this too.

Again, as you do this exercise, don't try to change the way you are breathing right now in any way. What you will be changing in this exercise is where you focus your attention. Using the steps below, first, you will practice focusing your attention on your nose. Then, you will focus on your chest. Take your time doing each step. Each step is a useful and important part of calming yourself.

Focus on the sensations of breathing at the tip of your nose. Breathing in and out through your nose, focus your attention on the physical sensations of the air moving in and out of your nostrils at the tip of your nose. Close your eyes, if you wish to.

As you breathe in, notice the sensation of air moving into your nose. How does it feel? Notice the temperature of the air. Listen to any sound that the air makes as it comes into your nose. As you breathe out, notice the sensation of air moving out of your nose. Don't try to force more air out than usual; just let the out-breath take as long as it takes. You might notice a slight change in the temperature of the air as you breathe out, because the inside of your body has warmed the air. You might also notice a soft sound as your breath moves out through your nose.

Continue breathing, focusing on the sensations at the tip of your nose. Are you surprised that there is so much to experience and learn simply as you breathe? While you are doing this exercise, you will find that you naturally become more relaxed on each out-breath. You are practicing your ability to calm yourself every time you move your attention to the sensations of your breath moving in and out.

Focus on the sensations of breathing in your chest. Keep breathing naturally, then shift your attention so that you start noticing sensations in your chest area. Focus your attention on the physical sensations of breathing that you can notice in this part of your body.

As you breathe in, notice how your chest rises. Notice how your shoulders seem to float upward. As you breathe out, notice how your chest falls back down. Feel your shoulders moving downward. Notice any sensations of relaxation in your body that are present as you breathe out. Breathing out brings a natural sense of calm and relaxation to the body, which you will probably notice.

You can focus on your breathing for as long as you wish. You can do it many times each day. In doing so, you are learning and practicing the skills of paying attention and relaxing through breathing.

Now that you have practiced calming yourself by *focusing on your breath* without changing it in any way, here are some exercises for you to do using your imagination to play with your breath. In each exercise, you will imagine a different situation. Notice the different sensations in your body with each experience, and use your breath to help you stay calm while you are doing this.

Exercise 1.2: "Snow Breathing"

Focus your attention on the air moving in and out of your nose. Close your eyes if you wish to, and imagine that snow is falling lightly all around you.

Concentrate on your in-breaths. Every time you breathe in, imagine crisp, frozen air entering your nose and filling spaces in your head with an exciting sensation of being "wide awake."

Let yourself fully experience this "wide awake" sensation as you breathe in and out three times, noticing the feeling of "awake" each time you breathe in and the feeling of calm each time you breathe out.

If you want to play more with this, imagine big crunchy snowflakes coating parts of your body, shining in the sunlight as more flakes swirl beautifully around you, while you breathe in crisp, cold air. Does this imagery make you feel like smiling?

When some people get nervous, they feel hot and sweaty, even on a cold day. If this happens to you when you are about to go somewhere, such as to the movies with a friend, you might choose to play with "snow breathing." Imagining the coolness of the snow while focusing on your breathing will help you calm down.

Exercise 1.3: "Breeze Breathing"

Begin by breathing the way you did when you focused on your chest in exercise 1.1, feeling the sensation of your chest rising and falling as your breath flows in and out of your body. Now, focus your attention on the sound of your breathing. Does it sound somewhat like a soft breeze? Close your eyes if you wish to, and imagine that the air you are breathing in is a soft breeze. Can you feel the softness in your chest?

Notice the different sounds the air makes as it goes in and out. Notice the sensations of softness filling your chest as it expands on every in-breath.

Imagine that you are standing or sitting in a comfortable spot while a light breeze is blowing.

Breathe in and out naturally.

Listen for the sounds of your breathing. Feel the softness of the breeze.

Let the sounds and sensations of your breathing calm your mind and body.

Any time that you feel too crowded or "closed in," "breeze breathing" can help you relax and open to feel the soft breeze flowing through you. For example, if you suddenly start to feel nervous while trying to get to your locker in a crowded hallway at school, focusing on the sounds of your breathing while imagining feeling a soft, gentle breeze might help you become calm and relaxed as you find your way.

You can now use the sounds and sensations of your body—what happens naturally—to help you relax. Any time that you want to calm down, remember that you can just focus your mind on your breathing. You can use your imagination to play with calming images in your mind, such as images of crisp snow or a soft breeze.

Have fun playing with these exercises. The more you practice, the more fun it will be and the easier it will be for you to use your breath to calm yourself whenever you feel nervous, even if you aren't nervous about anything in particular.

Chapter 2

soar with your butterflies: calm your anxiety

Every school day, when Jordan wakes up, she thinks about going to math class and gets a sick feeling in her stomach. Math is her best subject, and she loves numbers. She just gets panicky about being called on to say her answers out loud. It isn't as if she is nervous all the time, but she hates drawing attention to herself and seeing people look at her when she has to answer the teacher's questions. It's not even about whether she knows the right answer, because she almost always does. Maybe knowing so much about math makes it worse, because she is always being called on. She just wants to disappear. But she can't.

Jordan's mother calls the sick feeling in her stomach "butterflies" and says that Jordan should just relax and the butterflies will go away, but Jordan doesn't know how to do that. If she stays home because of this sick feeling, her mother might make her go to the doctor. But she feels that if she does go to school, she might throw up. What can she do?

Like Jordan, you have probably felt jittery sensations in your belly when you are anxious or worried or scared about something specific you need to do, such as go to a school dance or a family party or give a performance. Everyone feels this kind of sensation from time to time, usually because of worry or stress, but sometimes because of something exciting. The common name for this sensation is "butterflies in your stomach," because it feels as if a bunch of butterflies are fluttering around inside of you. Even though this is a normal sensation, it is quite understandably uncomfortable.

You might get butterflies in your stomach when you are getting ready to do something in the presence of a lot of other people who might be watching. You might get them when you are about to do something you have never tried before, or when you have to go into a new situation. You might get them when you have to speak in front of a group or give a performance. Sometimes people call this "stage fright."

When you have butterflies in your stomach, you probably feel as though the last thing you want to do is the thing that is making you feel nervous and uncomfortable. Like Jordan, you might worry that you are going to throw up. If you pay attention to the rest of your body, you may notice that you don't just feel like throwing up—your heart is beating faster, and your hands are feeling shaky too.

The good news is that there is a way to calm your butterflies. Noticing the butterflies—just observing that there is a fluttery feeling in your stomach—is the first step in being able to calm them. Then, you can do a deep breathing exercise to calm yourself.

Try the following exercise the next time that you feel jittery, fluttery, nervous sensations in your belly. (The "belly" is often called the abdomen or tummy; it includes your stomach and the area around and under your belly button.)

Exercise 2.1: Breathing with the Flutters

Sit down or lie down in a comfortable position. Close your eyes, if you wish to.

Place your hands gently on your belly, with your fingers resting right over your belly button.

Your usual tendency when you get butterflies in your stomach is probably to try not to feel those fluttering sensations. For this exercise, do exactly the opposite. Focus your attention on the sensations in your belly, and try to let yourself feel them even more. Let those sensations settle into your awareness, and start noticing how they change from moment to moment.

Breathe in deeply and let your belly expand so that it can have enough space for the nervous sensations. Don't try to stop the sensations.

Then, breathe out, at a long, slow pace.

Breathe in deeply and breathe out slowly at least three more times.

Notice a peaceful feeling when the fluttering starts to calm down.

It is a scientific fact that your body calms down naturally when you breathe deeply and slowly. When you gently rest your hands on your belly, you can notice your body calming down. You can practice resting your hands on your belly and breathing deeply at times when you aren't feeling particularly jittery, just to get used to doing it. Try it any time that you want to relax. The more you practice, the better your body will know how to calm itself, and the better you will feel.

Remember, getting butterflies in your stomach is normal—we all get them from time to time when we are stressed, nervous, or excited. Sometimes it is hard to tell what is giving you butterflies—stress, nerves, or excitement, or some combination of these things. All you know is you feel jittery. But, once you calm down, you might start to feel more energetic than nervous. So, when you have calmed the butterflies in your stomach, you can figure out whether you are excited or nervous, and then figure out what might work for you in the situation. When you calm your butterflies, you can use their energy in a different way—to fuel your curiosity about what is really going on and what you can do about it. You will be able to focus more on what you might actually like about the event or the job you have to do that is on your mind.

Here is an interesting fact: your brain has a direct connection to the nerves inside your belly. So, if you are freaking out or stressing out, your nervous thoughts will give you jittery, upset sensations in your belly; once you have calmed your body, you will notice that your mind is calmer too. When your mind is calm, you are free to choose to feel excited about the chance to meet new people on the first day of school, for example, or to feel excited to hear your favorite band at a school dance, even if you are sure you hate dancing. This feeling of excitement is the transformation of the fluttering of butterflies in your stomach into energy that you feel in your whole body—energy you can use to do what you want, even if you are a little scared about doing it.

Here is a way to focus the energy of your butterflies to fuel your *own* flight:

Exercise 2.2: Fueling Your Flight

Stop whatever you are doing. Make your body be still for a moment.

Settle and calm your butterflies using deep breathing. Take at least three deep breaths on purpose.

Think about whatever it is you are about to do that caused your butterflies. What is it that you really want? Try to use the energy of your butterflies to fuel your action. For example, you have designed an electrical project for science class that works exactly the way you want it to, but you are filled with butterflies because you have to present it in front of the group. You can calm the flutters and notice that you might be feeling excited. You are probably excited about the project. You might even be excited about telling people about it because it is so cool. You can use the energy of your butterflies and the excitement you have about your project to feel strong enough to choose to do the presentation anyway.

Remember Jordan, from the beginning of the chapter? Jordan learned to transform the energy of her butterflies into excitement about how much fun it was to solve math problems in her head so that she was less worried about what might happen in math class.

For anything new that sets your butterflies in motion, focus on what you might really get out of whatever is making you nervous. Could what is making you nervous be something that turns out to be fun? By focusing your mind on what you want, you can choose to calm your butterflies and turn their energy into sensations of excitement. If you make this your habit whenever you get a chance to try something new that looks a little scary but interesting, you will have more energy and more fun.

Chapter 3

create a pause button: get comfortable

Being around people who are talking and laughing together in the hallway at school is always awkward for Matt. He wants to join in, but the closer he gets to the group, the more nervous he gets. He doesn't know what to say, but he feels as if he has to say something. He can't just stand there and do nothing! So, he tries to do what he thinks the other people are doing: he starts laughing and talking about what he saw on TV last night. Usually a few people in the group turn to look at him but then look away and continue talking with each other—so he laughs louder and starts talking again. Then he feels even more nervous, so he just walks away as fast as he can.

You may feel nervous, just like Matt, when you want to join a group or try to talk to someone you would like to meet. You might not feel comfortable just standing around with other people. When you feel uncomfortable, you might grow jittery and talk nonstop, or laugh too loud, or move around a lot.

The exercises in this chapter will teach you how to pause on purpose so that you can get more comfortable with doing nothing. You can learn to pause and wait without feeling as if you have to jump in and be "social" right away. You will feel and look less nervous. You will feel and look more comfortable. And when you look more comfortable, people will actually feel more comfortable being around you.

Your mind, and everyone's mind, is very busy, filled with thoughts running around all the time. You may even be busy running around doing things all the time. When you read a book, you might rush through the pages as fast as you can. When you are talking, sometimes you might keep talking, even if you have a feeling you should stop!

Many teens on the autism spectrum don't yet know that they have a "pause button" that they can use to help them slow down. The idea of a personal pause button is like the pause button on a DVD player or on a video game. Creating a pause button for yourself in the following exercise will help you feel comfortable in many different social situations. You will find that being with other people is a different experience when you are using your pause button.

Exercise 3.1: Pause and Relax

For this exercise, you will need some room to walk around. Try it in your bedroom or in the backyard, for example.

Begin by standing or sitting still. Close your eyes, if you wish to. Breathe in; while you are breathing in, say the word "pause" in your mind. Breathe out; while you are breathing out, say the word "relax" in your mind.

Breathe in (saying "pause" in your mind) and breathe out (saying "relax" in your mind), slowly, two more times.

If you were sitting, stand up. If your eyes were closed, open them. Begin to walk slowly and look around you. After a while, perhaps one minute (which is about six breath cycles), stop walking, stand still, and focus on your breath, again saying to yourself "pause" on each in-breath and "relax" on each out-breath.

After three breath cycles, start walking again, but faster. Keep a gentle awareness of your breathing while you are walking faster.

At some point, make a decision to press your pause button and stop walking again. While you are paused, take one to three breaths. You will notice that you are naturally focusing your attention more on your breathing. Some people call this mindful breathing. You are using your mind to be aware of your breathing by focusing your attention on it. When you are able to pause and use mindful breathing, you will become more relaxed and comfortable being around others in various situations, even if you don't actually join in with them.

By pausing, you allow your body and mind to naturally begin to relax and settle into a feeling of greater comfort and ease. This comfort and ease is known as the "relaxation response." Your body naturally has this relaxation response when you are able to pause and breathe in and out slowly. The relaxation response reduces stress and anxiety, and it helps settle your body and mind.

By practicing this pause during your usual "fast forward" action around other people, you will notice feeling more comfortable—whether you try talking, joining an activity, or just hanging out.

We usually think of "power" in terms of something moving with a lot of energy, but when you are nervously moving around, you probably don't feel very powerful at all. In this next exercise, you are going to play with creating nervous energy on purpose and then making your own personal pause button. You will gain a feeling of power when you learn to use your pause button. When you feel some of this power, you will feel more in control of yourself and more able to make decisions about when or whether to join or speak up in a social situation. You won't just be reacting from your nervousness.

Exercise 3.2: The Power of the Pause

First, create some nervous energy. Make your body really jittery. Jump around, scratch your head, and fidget with your fingers. Shake your feet and wiggle your arms. Clap as if you are applauding a great show. Start talking out loud, about anything, even if it doesn't make sense. Maybe you could talk about a movie you like or your favorite food. It doesn't really matter. Just keep talking. If you feel like laughing, do it.

Now, get ready to pause. How you signal yourself that you are choosing to press your "pause" button is up to you. You might imagine the pause symbol (usually two vertical lines) that appears on your screen. Or you might see the word "pause" in your mind. Or you could say the word "pause" out loud. As soon as you press your "pause" button, stop all action right away. Stop moving your body. Stop talking. Stand still.

Congratulations! You have successfully operated your pause button. Notice how this pause feels. Really take the time to notice any sensations in your body.

- Do you feel tingling in your fingers or arms?
- What do you feel as you breathe?
- Notice any sounds around you; if there are none, notice the silence.
- Notice how your face feels.
- Notice the sensations in the soles of your feet.

There is energy and power in all of these sensations. When you pause, you collect and store your energy instead of using it up right away. Your energy is still there, ready to be used whenever you decide to use it. You have moved from nervous energy, which drains your power, to the power of being still—the power of the pause. It may not make sense that there is energy in stillness, but practice using your pause button, and you will get to feel the power of this energy inside of yourself.

Practicing these exercises will give you more control and power when you are around other people in situations that make you feel awkward or uncomfortable. For example, you might feel like jumping into a conversation about a new video game as soon as you hear it mentioned, without waiting to hear what others are saying about it. Jumping in without pausing might make the other people annoyed or uncomfortable, because you talk about it so quickly and so much. Talking quickly and without stopping might be a sign that you are feeling nervous, and this is a good time to use your pause button.

Learning how to pause and slow down gives you a chance to get used to hanging around the group, and it lets others get used to your being around them. A pause is not the same thing as a stop. A pause is a break in the action, with more to come; a stop is just that—an end. A pause contains energy ready to use, under your control. People will be more comfortable around you if they know that you have control over your own energy. It will be easier for you to connect with others and for them to connect with you if you have practiced creating and using your pause button.

Chapter 4

light the stage: choose the best focus

One day, Ben wanted to hang out in the art room, where everyone was laughing and having a good time. But, as soon as he went into the art room, he felt nervous and uncomfortable. He went straight to the one computer he always used, and he worked on his designs. He hardly ever looked up to see what was going on around him. He didn't even notice when people came over to look at his designs.

Even though Ben wanted to be where people looked as if they were having fun, he didn't feel relaxed about hanging out with anybody once he got there. He thought nobody was interested in his artwork, but he didn't even notice when people did come over to see what he was doing. He was so focused on his computer screen that he didn't see what was really happening in the room. It was as if nothing existed but what was right in front of him. So, he continued to feel that nobody cared about his artwork, which kept him feeling kind of stressed, even though he liked what he was doing.

You may not realize that you sometimes focus on details or certain objects in a situation and don't see the whole picture. This is what was happening to Ben. Do you think this might happen to you, too? If you don't see the whole picture, you might misunderstand what's going on around you and jump to negative conclusions, especially in a social situation. Social situations are complicated, with many things happening at once. When people only see one part of the picture, or one piece of the action, it is even harder to grasp what is happening.

You may have a tendency to focus more on certain details because of something that you are particularly interested in, like Ben and his designs on the computer. The exercises in this chapter will teach you how to take in more information about the whole scene—everything that is going on around you—so that you don't miss something that is useful to know. Knowing more about what's happening around you will help you feel calmer. You might learn more about how to join in with a group, if that is something you want to do.

In the following exercise, you will practice two basic ways to notice what's going on around you. We call these two ways "spotlight attention" and "floodlight attention."

Spotlight attention focuses on one particular part of the scene very clearly and brightly and stays in that one place for a long time without moving. This is a very good kind of attention to use for some things, such as doing homework, solving a math problem, or playing a computer game. You are probably really good at using this way of paying attention.

Floodlight attention lights up the whole scene, allowing you to see everything that is going on. You may not be aware of the times when you use floodlight attention, but you probably do use it already in certain situations—for example, when you walk into a crowded movie theater and look for an empty seat.

For this exercise, you will use your mind to notice and pay attention to your surroundings. You will practice some simple ways to notice which kind of attention you are using at any given time. Your mind is always paying attention to something, unless you are in a deep sleep. And where you place your attention is a choice—*your choice.*

Exercise 4.1: Spotlight Attention vs. Floodlight Attention

To practice spotlight attention, hold up your right hand in front of your face so that you are looking at the palm of your hand. Look at every little crease in the palm of your hand. Look at the details of the shape of your palm—the folds, the bumpy parts, and the flat parts. Keep your attention focused on the palm of your hand for a whole minute. If your mind wanders to other thoughts or things in the room, simply bring your attention gently back to the palm of your hand. You can think of using spotlight attention as "zooming in."

Now, to practice floodlight attention, slowly walk all around your house. As you enter each room, stop for a moment and scan the whole room, trying to notice as much as you can without focusing for too long on one particular person or thing. You might notice sounds, you might notice the temperature of the air, you might notice colors and shadows, or you might notice people. Think of using floodlight attention as "zooming out." You can practice floodlight attention many times a day. Each time you walk into a new room, a new space, or a new situation, stop for a moment and look all around to notice what is there: the people, the furniture, the objects on the shelves and walls, everything around you. If you aren't used to doing this, you might be surprised at how much fun it can be to see so much.

You are probably zoomed-in (using spotlight attention) most of the time. You probably have a very good ability to focus on details. The following two-part exercise will help you develop the skill of noticing and understanding more of a whole picture (zooming out). You will be able to understand the whole picture from learning more about all its parts, similar to putting a jigsaw puzzle together.

Being able to zoom in and zoom out helps people get more comfortable in social situations because they can see what's going on in the whole room. It helps people know how to fit into or avoid different groups more easily. So, learning to move from "pixels to pictures" can be a useful skill to practice as part of getting calmer.

Exercise 4.2: Moving from Pixels to Pictures

Part 1. Find a large photograph of a person's face from a newspaper or magazine. Hold it in your hands. Bring it very close to your face, and focus your eyes on a small detail of the person's face, perhaps the mouth. Try to make a guess about what this person was feeling at the time the picture was taken, from looking at just this one little part of his or her body.

Now, imagine that the detail you are looking at is a pixel—a tiny dot that combines with many other tiny dots to make a picture. Your job in this part of the exercise is to learn how that pixel is actually part of a picture, so that you learn to broaden your perspective in any situation. So, slowly move the picture away from your face and watch how the "pixels" gather together to make a whole picture. Does the whole picture give you different information than what you guessed from looking at the "pixel"?

Part 2. Stand in front of a full-length mirror and examine your own reflection. Zoom in on just one detail, such as your mouth, and try not to see anything else but that (use spotlight attention). Now, zoom out (use floodlight attention), and see how the mouth is part of the whole face, and how the face is part of the head, and how the head is at the top of the whole body. Notice how the "pixels" fit together to create the whole image of you.

Then practice zooming back in and zooming back out to rehearse the skill of broadening your perspective.

You are learning how to use this tool (flexible attention) to help you get more comfortable when you decide to try hanging out with other people. When you see a group of people you would like to join—your family, perhaps, or your classmates at school—but you feel nervous and unsure about what to do, practice zooming out so that you can gather all the information in the situation. Then, you will be able to see whether they are looking your way, or bunched together in a tight circle, or moving around getting food, or getting ready to leave. When you have more information, you will be better able to figure out what you should do.

Chapter 5

groove with gravity: feel solid in your body

Hannah's mind is always filled with thoughts and pictures. When people ask her questions, she gets flustered and can't decide what to say in response because so much is going on in her mind. Sometimes her body feels kind of weird and shaky when she gets confused like this. She is always nervous, not knowing what to say or do. She worries about what other people might say to her, and she worries about what she should say to other people. She just doesn't know a way to settle down and give her mind a rest.

Sometimes, you may feel nervous as Hannah does. When you feel nervous, your "buzzing" mind is filled with thoughts, and you might begin to feel confused. When your thoughts are racing around in your mind, it can make you feel jumpy. At times like this, you are living too much in your mind and not enough in your body. In fact, you may actually forget that you have a body. You need to remember your body to help settle your mind. This is called "getting grounded" or "grounding yourself" because it can make your body feel as solid and strong as the ground that you are standing on, and can keep your thoughts from running off with your mind.

The natural gravitational pull of the Earth holds you (and everybody else) anchored to the ground. So, grounding yourself means focusing your attention on how gravity anchors your body to the ground and helps you feel solid.

One way to feel grounded is to focus your attention on the center of your body while you breathe. Your center is in the middle of your body, around your waist or belly button. Try the following exercise anywhere and at any time. You can choose to keep your eyes open for this exercise; however, closing them might help you focus on the sensations in your body without being distracted by what's going on outside of you.

Exercise 5.1: Grounding Yourself in the Center of Your Body

Stand (or sit) still. Pause. Take a deep breath. Close your eyes, if you wish to.

Notice how the force of the Earth's gravity holds you on the ground where you are standing or pulls you down into your seat, if you are sitting in a chair.

Rest your hands on your belly. Notice the feeling of your hands resting on your belly.

Keep your hands resting comfortably on your belly and focus your attention on your breathing.

Notice how your breathing can help you relax. By focusing your attention on your breathing in the center of your body, you can feel more solid in your whole body.

Notice how your body can start to feel more solid and anchored to the ground.

Try this simple exercise the next time that you are stuck in your thoughts. By focusing your attention on the center of your body, you are taking your attention away from your buzzing thoughts. Moving your attention to the center of your body and away from your thoughts can help give you a solid, grounded feeling. This is very calming. You will feel less confused, and your mind will begin to feel settled.

Now that you have practiced grounding yourself in the center of your body while standing up or sitting in a chair, try this next exercise when you are lying down. Remember, you will be using your breathing as a tool. This is a great exercise to try with your eyes closed, because it can be very relaxing.

Exercise 5.2: Grooving with Gravity

Sometimes, it is fun to do this exercise with something small and lightweight that you can place on your belly. You might have an old stuffed animal or even a Frisbee that you can use for this purpose. Try it and see whether you like the way it feels.

Lie down in a comfortable place. Lie on your back so that you are facing the ceiling or the sky. Close your eyes, if you wish to.

Notice how the force of gravity holds your body steady on the floor or ground (if you are outside). Let your body relax and sink into this force of gravity. You can think of this as letting your body groove with gravity.

Rest one or both of your hands on your belly.

Now, focus your attention on the physical sensations of breathing that you can notice in your belly. Notice how the center of your body rises slightly as you breathe in. As you breathe out, notice how your belly sinks back down.

Breathe in and out, with your attention focused on the rising and sinking of your belly, as many times as you wish. You will feel your body becoming more relaxed with each out-breath. You are also developing your concentration skills every time you deliberately put your attention on the slight rising and sinking of your belly as you breathe.

The next time that you know you are going to be in a situation where you will feel under pressure, such as having to be in a debate for class or having to rush to catch the bus in the morning, focus on your center of gravity and your breathing as a way to calm yourself and prepare for the situation. Feeling solid and centered and grounded in your body will be surprisingly soothing, even if you still have trouble finding the right words or gathering everything you need to bring to school.

In the next exercise, you will use your imagination along with your breathing to help you feel grounded and solid in your body. Have fun playing with this different way of feeling grounded.

Exercise 5.3: "Sun Breathing"

Find a comfortable place to lie down. Lie on your back, with one or both of your hands resting comfortably on your belly. Close your eyes, if you wish to.

Breathe in and out. Feel the weight and temperature of your hands on your belly. Notice the way that your belly rises when you breathe in and sinks down when you breathe out. Focus on the sensation of your belly relaxing when you breathe out. Notice if you are picturing anything in your mind. Notice if you see any colors or shapes. Notice any feeling of warmth.

As you continue to breathe slowly and restfully, imagine that you are outdoors on a warm summer day. If you want, you can imagine that your hands are the sun, and rays of sunshine are flowing from your hands over your body at exactly the temperature that is right for you. Feel the sensations of the sun radiating warmth. Continue breathing in and out.

Notice if your hands actually begin to feel warmer from the sunshine and the relaxation.

You can try "sun breathing" whenever you are feeling adrift and maybe even a little scared. When people get nervous or scared, they can get a chilly feeling. If you get chilly like that when you are nervous, you might prefer this particular way of getting grounded. Resting with the sensations of breathing while imagining the warm sun can make you feel better and give you new energy in a relaxed, calm way.

Part II

Use Your Thoughts and Feelings to Build Your Independence

Chapter 6

your body is the actor: identify your feelings

Charlie is always thinking about something. He is so busy thinking that he doesn't really notice the people and things around him. Often, he is thinking about an interesting math problem.

Charlie is so busy thinking interesting thoughts that he doesn't even notice his body and what might be going on with it. So, he doesn't know when he is tired, cold, or hungry. He doesn't realize that the way his body feels can affect his thoughts. Being hungry, for example, can make it harder to solve a math problem. He also doesn't usually know what mood he is in. Mood can affect thoughts as well. If he doesn't notice that he is in a "bad" mood, he doesn't know why he is having more trouble than usual writing the first paragraph of an essay, for example.

How can Charlie become more aware of his body and his feelings? He can use his body to give him information about how he is feeling. In this chapter, you will learn to pay attention to what's going on in your body in order to learn more about your feelings (emotions).

Sometimes you might not know what you are feeling, which makes it hard to know what another person might be feeling. What you will learn from this chapter is to get in touch with what you are feeling by noticing the sensations in your body. This practice will also be useful later, when we look at clues as to what other people are feeling.

The following exercise will help you notice sensations in your body that can alert you to your feelings. Give yourself two minutes to do this exercise. Use a computer, a watch, a cell phone, or another device with a timer that you can set for two minutes. You can try closing your eyes for this exercise so that you can focus more on the sensations in your body and not be distracted by what's going on outside of you.

Exercise 6.1: Noticing What's Going On in Your Body

Sit in your favorite place (for example, in your favorite chair, on your bed, or on the floor). Close your eyes, if you wish to.

Focus on sensations in your body. You can start by focusing on the top of your head and then slowly moving your attention down through your face, shoulders, chest, belly, legs, and feet.

Try to feel curious about what you might notice in your body sensations. Here are some questions that might help you become more aware of sensations in your body. Consider each question, then take a moment to see what you notice. You may not notice anything, and that is okay.

- Do you notice any places in your body that are calm and relaxed?
- Do you notice any places in your body that are jumpy or jittery?
- Do you notice any places in your body that feel tight or tense?
- Do you notice any places in your body that feel warm or cool?
- Do you notice what your face is doing—for example, is it smiling, frowning, or relaxed?
- Do you notice what your hands are doing—for example, are they open, closed, clenched, or relaxed?

Other sensations that you might notice include itches and twitches. Just keep noticing everything going on in your body for two minutes. When you focus on your body, you will notice that there are many different kinds of sensations going on in your body all the time and that body sensations are always changing. They come and go, just as thoughts come and go.

After two minutes, stand up, stretch, and take a deep breath.

Often, your body sensations are connected to your feelings. Feelings are sometimes called emotions. In this book, we will just call them feelings. When you notice what's going on in your body, you will learn more about your feelings.

In the next exercise, you will pretend to be an actor who has been given three different feelings to play. You will be using specific parts of your body—your face, arms, and hands—to portray three basic feelings that everybody has: sad, mad, and glad. This might seem confusing at first, but if you just follow the directions, you may find this exercise fun and interesting.

Exercise 6.2: Trying on Different Feelings

Stand in front of a full-length mirror so that you can see your entire body.

Trying on the "mad" feeling. Start with your face:

1. Clench your teeth.
2. Push your head forward a bit.
3. Narrow your eyes so that you are peering out through little slits.
4. Notice that your eyebrows come down and pull together.
5. Look at your face in the mirror, and make it look as mad as you can.

While keeping your mad face on, focus on your hands and arms:

1. Make your hands into tight fists.

2. Notice how the energy in your fists goes right up your arms.
3. Bend your arms at the elbows, keeping your fists clenched.
4. Notice the sensations in your body. Do you feel tightness in your muscles, do you feel pressure in your belly, or do you feel your breathing quickening? These are some of the body sensations of feeling mad.

Now, drop the "mad" act and return to your normal self. Shake out your arms and hands. Yawn (or pretend to yawn) to relax your face. Loosen yourself up, getting ready to try on the next feeling.

Trying on the "sad" feeling. Start with your face:

1. Pull the corners of your mouth down as far as you can.
2. Notice that the outside corners of your eyes start to pull down a little bit.
3. Lower your chin so it kind of sinks into your neck.
4. Look at your face in the mirror, and try to make your eyes look sad.

While keeping your sad face on, focus on your hands and arms:

1. Let your shoulders slump down.
2. Let your hands go limp, as if you can't even hold anything with them.
3. Let your arms feel heavy so that they hang straight down against your sides.

4. Let all the muscles in your arms go limp.
5. Notice the sensations in your face, with its pulled-down mouth, and throughout your limp hands and arms. These are some of the body sensations that go with sad feelings.

Now, shake off the "sad" act, just as you did the "mad" act. Now you are ready to try on a glad feeling.

Trying on the "glad" feeling. "Glad" is a feeling of being happy. To try on feeling glad, start with your face:

1. Smile at yourself in the mirror. At first, this might feel false, like having to pose for a photo you would rather not be in!
2. Start playing with different kinds of smiles. This might end up feeling silly, which is helpful, since you are trying on cheerful feelings.
3. A real smile creates wrinkles at the outside corners of the eyes. Try to achieve this effect.
4. Just pulling up the corners of your mouth into the shape of a smile (even if it feels kind of fake) actually creates sensations in your body that help make you feel happy for real.

While keeping your glad face on, focus on your hands and arms:

1. Stretch out your fingers and open your hands.
2. Lift up your arms, keeping your hands open.
3. Look in the mirror to see your body showing the feeling of being happy.

4. Notice the sensations in your smiling face and in your uplifted arms and open hands. These are some of the body sensations that go with feeling glad.

As you have probably figured out, different feelings create different sensations in your body.

You can do this exercise as often as you wish. This will give you practice in noticing sensations in your body so that you can more easily tell what you are feeling. Experiment with other feelings. Each time you try on feelings, be sure to end by acting "glad," to help you feel good afterward.

Everyone around you experiences the same feelings as you do at one time or another. In other words, your feelings are the same kinds of feelings that the people around you may have. So, while you are noticing your own feelings, you are also noticing feelings that other people may have that are just like yours. Learning about your feelings can help you understand what you have in common with other people. Then what other people do and say will make more sense to you. This can help you understand how to connect with others, when you choose to reach out and do so.

Chapter 7

the astonishing energy of feelings: use your feelings as power

Noah was so used to feeling frustrated that he never imagined another way to respond to disappointment. One day, for example, Noah was looking forward to having his favorite ice cream—caramel fudge—from the ice cream store. But when he got to the store, he found that they had run out of that flavor. Noah became frustrated, and it got even worse, because the more Noah tried to stop feeling frustrated, the more frustrated he got!

What Noah really needed was a way to calm down enough to gain control of his feelings and use the power of his feelings (his frustration) to take positive action.

Often, you might not be aware of your feelings, even though they are swirling around inside you all the time. You might not know that you are having a certain feeling until it explodes out of your body as words, tears, or hurtful actions. Feelings have astonishing power. Sometimes, they can completely stress you out. However, you can learn to use your emotional energy to change the way you feel, instead of staying upset and ending up feeling bad. For example, frustration can give you the power to fix a problem, and sadness can give you the power to show kindness.

Try the following exercise to get to know the different powers that your feelings have.

Exercise 7.1: Feeling Power

Frustration. The next time you are feeling frustrated, pay attention to what your body feels like doing, because it probably feels like taking action.

- Do you feel like yelling or shouting?
- Do your hands and arms feel like moving?
- Do your legs feel like running?

Notice the sensations. Then, you can use the power of your frustration to take positive action for yourself. For example, when you notice that you feel like yelling, you can take a moment to ask yourself what you really want to say, and then use the energy of your frustration to express yourself clearly and firmly.

Sadness. The next time you are feeling sad, notice the sensations in your face, chest, and belly.

- Do your eyes feel like crying?
- Does your belly feel soft and sensitive?
- Does your chest feel heavy?

Notice any sensations you have while you feel sad. You might even feel the wetness of tears on your face if you are crying. Do you feel sorry for yourself? Sometimes people will tell you that it is wrong to feel sorry for yourself, but when you feel sorry for yourself, you are really feeling kindness and tenderness toward yourself. The power in your sadness is actually kindness! You can use the power of sadness to be kind to yourself. Letting yourself feel your sad feelings is a way of being kind to yourself.

Happiness. The next time that you are laughing about something, such as a joke or a funny show, pay attention to how your body feels. You may notice your face is stretched into a big smile. Sometimes people laugh so hard, they feel tears coming out of their eyes. Have you ever heard of a belly laugh? Sometimes when people laugh, they feel their bellies move. Does this happen to you?

Feelings can be like wild horses. If you're not in charge of your feelings, they can run away and take you with them.

On the other hand, you and your feelings can become partners. Just as a horseback rider can guide a horse, you can direct the power of your feelings. Here are some exercises to practice when you have powerful feelings. These activities enlist your imagination to help you use the power of your feelings in positive ways. These exercises may feel kind of funny at first, but just try them out and see what you discover.

Exercise 7.2: Using the Powers of Your Feelings

Frustration. When you notice that you are feeling frustrated, imagine that you are a little bird. You are scavenging for scraps of food left on the ground, but all the other birds are snatching up the scraps of food before you can. It would be a wise little bird that would fly away to look for food somewhere else.

Frustration is a call to action. Use the energy you feel in your frustration to take positive action. Noah (from the beginning of the chapter) could have used the action energy of his frustration to go to another store to look for his favorite ice cream flavor, instead of staying stuck in his frustration. Can you do something similar?

Sadness. When you notice that you are feeling sad, imagine that you are a little puppy left alone standing by the door waiting for your human friend to come home from school. Imagine yourself (as yourself) using your kindness to make the puppy (who is also yourself) feel less sad. You could pet the puppy and give the puppy fresh water. You could take the puppy for a walk. You could say kind words to the puppy.

In the same way, you can be kind to yourself to help you feel less sad. You can brush your hair. You can get something to drink. You can do something that you enjoy. You can say kind words to yourself. You can take care of yourself in kind ways, the way you would be kind to a sad little puppy.

Happiness. When you notice that you are feeling happy, imagine that you are a kitten full of curiosity and playfulness. Anything—a button, a string, a leaf, a twig—can become a toy. Anything that moves is something to pounce on and play with. All you want to do is keep playing every minute.

Stay with that happy feeling, and enjoy yourself every minute, like the kitten. Does imagining yourself as a kitten make you feel happier—make you feel like laughing? There is freedom in laughter and happiness. Enjoy the feeling. Some people say that laughter is the best medicine.

In this chapter, you have learned how to practice noticing your feelings by noticing the sensations in your body. In noticing the sensations of your feelings, you have also noticed how powerful they can be. You have practiced using your imagination to become more familiar with the power that your feelings have. Now, you can direct and manage the power of your feelings in positive ways.

Chapter 8

basic meltdown prevention: managing anger

George has a reputation in his family and at school for having an uncontrollable temper. He has angry meltdowns every day. He has no idea why these meltdowns happen or when they will happen.

For example, at dinnertime, sometimes George comes downstairs and smells what is for dinner and feels happy. Other times, he can't stand the smell of dinner cooking that drifts up to his bedroom, so he starts screaming that he isn't eating anything and isn't coming down for dinner.

George is always getting in trouble at school and with his parents as a result of these angry episodes. Some kids in his school sometimes pick on him to try to get him to explode. It usually works. As a result, other kids in school try to stay away from him because they are afraid that he might blow up at any time.

One of the biggest problems for George is that he doesn't really know what triggers his anger. He doesn't even know that he is angry right before he explodes—he doesn't notice his anger getting stronger. When he explodes, and people ask him why he is angry, he gets frustrated because he doesn't know. He doesn't even have words for what's going on with him because he is so agitated. And then when he says he doesn't know, people keep asking him more questions! This makes him even more angry, and he shuts down.

Maybe you can identify with George because you sometimes have meltdowns too. Meltdowns can happen when you are overwhelmed, usually by angry feelings. All teenagers have to deal with strong feelings, including strong angry feelings, because of an interesting fact about brain development: the part of the brain that helps people control strong feelings such as anger doesn't fully develop until at least age twenty. So, anger is kind of hard for all teenagers to handle, because the part of their brains that can help control strong feelings is not yet fully grown.

Teens with autism often say they find it hard to stop meltdowns from happening. They, and you, may have difficulty managing anger for many different reasons. You may feel overwhelmed in new situations, and that can make you feel frustrated. You might feel there is too much going on around you and you just want to be left alone. When you can't be alone as you want, you might feel frustrated. You might even grow angry. You may have a thought that gets stuck in your mind and keeps making you even angrier.

Anger is a useful and important feeling. Managing your anger does not mean holding it in or stuffing it down. It does not mean that you will never feel angry. The first step in managing your anger is learning to notice when you are angry. Then, you can determine how angry you are. Are you at 100 percent (full-blown rage)? Are you at 80 percent (really angry)? Are you at 50 percent (very frustrated)? Are you at 20 percent (annoyed)?

In this chapter, you will practice using your thoughts and feelings to prevent meltdowns. You might not realize it right now, but managing your anger and preventing meltdowns is a major way to be in charge of yourself and build your independence.

To manage your anger, you may need to do some detective work to find out the triggers for your anger. Take a moment right now to think about a time when you were feeling okay but then suddenly you felt very angry. Ask yourself the following questions:

- Did you have difficulty understanding what other people were talking about?
- Did someone disagree with you and you didn't see that person's point of view, or did you think that someone else's idea was wrong?
- Did you feel confused and stressed about what other people were doing?
- Did you have sensory overload from lights, colors, smells, tastes, or sounds that became overwhelming?

- Did someone bully you or pick on you?
- Did angry thoughts get stuck in your mind?

Each of these situations might be a trigger for your anger at different times. Do you think that any of these situations might have triggered George's angry reactions? Here is how you can gain more control over your angry feelings so that you don't end up having a meltdown so often, not even knowing how you got to that point.

Step 1: Watch for warning signs. Sometimes by the time you notice that you are angry, it is too late to do anything about it, and you don't want to cooperate with anyone because you are in anger mode. You are already having a meltdown. The problem is that you didn't realize that you were getting angry before your switch got flipped and there was no going back. So, catching yourself before you are in the middle of a meltdown is a new skill to learn. The most important step in being able to prevent a meltdown is knowing when it is starting to happen, right from the beginning.

Before you can catch yourself about to have a meltdown, you must learn to be aware of how your body feels when you are getting angry. Get to know the signs of anger in your body. Think about a time when you were really angry, and ask yourself these questions:

- Did you breathe faster?
- Did you clench your teeth?
- Were your shoulder muscles tight?

- Did you feel like running away?
- Did you feel like screaming?
- Did your face feel hot?
- Did you feel like punching something?
- Were you frowning?
- Did you feel your eyes getting narrow, like slits?

Practice getting to know how your body feels when you are angry. If you learn to look for the signs of anger in your body, the next time you notice them starting to arise, you can pause to choose what action to take before you become really angry, as described next.

Step 2: Decide not to have a meltdown. Just noticing the anger in your body won't automatically keep you from having a meltdown. You need to actually make a decision not to have a meltdown. This might seem odd, and it is harder than it sounds. It might be very difficult the first few times that you try it out.

When you decide not to have a meltdown, use either (or both) of the following as a way of managing your anger:

- Just breathe; don't speak. The simple action of not talking is a very powerful way of putting on the brakes when you feel angry.
- Walk away from the situation.

Step 3: Choose a distracting activity. The decision not to have a meltdown does not make the feeling of anger go away, so you will have to work hard and fast to stop a meltdown from happening. What will help you stop a meltdown from happening is choosing to do something else right away. Find something physically active to do with all of that emotional energy. Or do something creative. Or do something that is both active and creative. As a way of distracting yourself from your anger so that it doesn't overwhelm you, focus on something you like to do and do it. It may help to remember the formula MA = D x T, or Managing Anger = Distraction multiplied by the amount of Time spent doing the distraction. Choose the distraction that will work best in the situation. The amount of time that you will need to focus on the distraction in order to be successful in preventing a meltdown will depend on your level of anger. If the level of your anger is high, you might need to spend more time doing the distracting activity. If you have less anger, you may need less time.

Here are some "distractions" to try out. If one doesn't work so great, try another—see what works best for you.

- Pace back and forth. Or run around in circles. If you are inside a building, go outside to walk, if you can.
- Listen to music. Music that means something to you can help your mind and body calm down. This will help you feel more in charge of your feelings.
- Punch a pillow.
- Play your drums or your guitar or some other musical instrument.

- Do some rock climbing.
- Bake a huge batch of brownies or make a pasta sauce.
- Watch TV.
- Read a book.
- Fold origami.
- Do complex math problems in your head.
- Do a fun puzzle, such as Sudoku or KenKen.
- Practice "grounding yourself" in the soles of your feet (see the next exercise).
- Translate your anger into words about what you want (try the scripts in the next section).

It is always useful to carry distractions in your pocket or backpack. If you have an iPod or smartphone, load it up with puzzles or your favorite music. Keep some paper on hand, if you like folding origami. Or, carry a Rubik's cube wherever you go.

A powerful way to manage your anger and calm down is to practice focusing your attention on how your feet feel on the ground. This is another method of "grounding yourself," or feeling strong and solid in the very center of your body. Grounding yourself is a very important skill for managing anger. There are several kinds of exercises that will help you learn this skill.

The following quick exercise can help you take a short pause, settle into your body to feel strong and solid, and reduce any anger that you are feeling. You can think of this as exercising your concentration muscle to ground your energy and keep yourself centered and balanced, no matter what's going on around you. Use this exercise any time that you begin to notice that you are feeling angry, frustrated, or off-balance. You can also use it to reduce anxiety or fear, or you can just use it as a way to settle yourself before doing something or going somewhere.

Exercise 8.1: Grounding Yourself in the Soles of Your Feet

Stand still for a moment, take a deep breath, and focus your attention on the sensations in the soles (bottoms) of your feet. Close your eyes, if you wish to.

- If you are wearing socks and shoes, begin to notice the feeling of the fabric of your socks against the skin of your feet. Begin to notice the solid feeling of the soles of your feet against the insoles of your shoes. Try to feel the force of gravity anchoring your feet to the floor.

- If your feet are bare or you are just wearing socks: Begin to notice the feeling of your socks, the rug, or the floor against the skin of your feet. Begin to notice the solid feeling of the soles of your feet against whatever you are standing on, whether it is hard or soft. If you are outside—for example, in your backyard—notice how the soles of your feet feel against the grass or the pavement. Try to feel the force of gravity gently anchoring your feet to the ground.

Continue to focus on the sensations in the soles of your feet as you count slowly from one to thirty.

Now that you have practiced feeling the pull of gravity on the soles of your feet, you may feel more solid in your body. You can feel that your body is anchored solidly to the Earth. Next, you will use your imagination to play with two different feelings of being grounded, solid, and confident in your own body. Playing with the feeling of being grounded can strengthen your ability to ground yourself any time that you want to and help you feel comfortable when you are just standing around. In this exercise, you will imagine standing in two very different substances—first sand and then mud—so that you can explore different ways of feeling grounded. You may find this imaginative exercise kind of fun.

Exercise 8.2: Standing in Sand and Standing in Mud

Stand in a relaxed way. Focus your attention on the soles of your feet. Try to relax as fully as possible into the experience of gravity, the force that holds your feet to the floor so that you can stand up straight. Close your eyes, if you wish to.

Continue to focus on the sensations in the soles of your feet, letting your feet relax into the feeling of being safely and comfortably held by gravity, for a minute or two.

Sand. Imagine that you are standing, barefoot, in warm, soft, fine sand. Breathe into this feeling, and concentrate on imagining tiny grains of sand against the bottom of your feet. Try to imagine the sensations of the sand on your skin. Imagine how the sand shifts to fit your feet perfectly as your toes nestle into the sand. You may find yourself feeling very comfortable and solid in your body as you focus on these sensations at the bottom of your feet. Try breathing in and wiggling your toes. Imagine feeling the sand slide a bit between them, making the perfect fit even better. You might even feel like laughing or smiling. Rock just a bit forward on your toes and back on your heels, and imagine feeling the space your feet make in the sand. Breathe, and pay attention to the pleasant sensation of the sand cushioning the soles of your feet as you rock gently back and forth.

When you feel ready to try experiencing a different texture, take a deep breath, shake your feet one at a time, and know that you can return to the sand any time you want.

Mud. Imagine that you are standing in really thick, silky smooth mud. Imagine that you can feel your feet squishing down into the gooey mud, sinking down a little until the mud climbs up the sides of your feet and over the tops of your feet, like mud slippers.

Wiggle your toes, and imagine feeling the sensations. Spread out your toes a bit more and feel the warm, thick mud around them. Slowly, lift one foot slightly off the ground. Put that foot down, and then slowly lift the other. Feel the slight pull of the mud and the connection that it makes between the bottom of your foot and the ground.

Notice the sensations in your entire body as you stand there. You might feel relaxed and solid in your body while you anchor yourself in the gravity of mud. Move your feet slowly, and breathe in and out. What kinds of feelings do you have, and how do they change? Do you feel kind of silly? You might feel like smiling or laughing. Did you ever play in the mud as a child? Is it something that you enjoy or not? Just notice the way you feel about it; don't judge your feeling one way or another.

Now that you have done this exercise on your own, try it when you are standing around with other people. Does imagining that you are standing in sand or standing in mud help you feel more relaxed and confident?

With these imaginative exercises, you are teaching yourself how to have fun by relaxing into feeling grounded, which will be very useful in helping you calm yourself, manage your anger, and prevent meltdowns. You are learning to feel strong and solid while using your imagination, having fun, and being curious.

For "emergency meltdown prevention," you can prepare a list of phrases to memorize that you can use instead of hurtful words that you might say in anger when you are starting to have a meltdown. The following exercise will show you how. Just as you learn a foreign language by memorizing certain phrases to use in certain situations, this exercise is about translating the language of anger into phrases that can help you manage your anger.

Exercise 8.3: Translating the Language of Anger

Take a sheet of paper and divide it into two columns. In the first column, list things you might say when you react with anger. In the second column, translate your anger into words that other people can really understand so that the situation doesn't escalate into a meltdown. For example:

Column 1: Anger	Column 2: Managing Anger (translation)
"Everything is your fault."	"I'm feeling angry right now, and I want you to know how I'm feeling."
"I hate you."	"When you forget to give me my allowance, I feel really angry."
"You never give me what I want."	"I don't want to eat sushi. I want pizza."
"Leave me alone! You're ruining my life!"	"My feelings got hurt. I want to be alone for a while."
"I'm sick of you."	"I'm too upset right now to hang out with you anymore today."

When you know that you will be going into a situation that might make you angry, think of things you might blurt out in anger or things you usually say when you get upset so that you can be prepared with translations. Do this on a daily basis if it helps you. Creating translation lists such as this, even memorizing translated phrases and sentences, will add to all the skills you have been practicing to help you prevent meltdowns and manage your anger.

Here is a list of some other tips for managing your anger and preventing meltdowns, as well as reminders of some things we have covered in this chapter:

- When you are having trouble understanding what other people are feeling or thinking, ask a question.
- When you are having difficulty seeing a situation from somebody else's point of view, use your breath and your imagination to "ground yourself," and keep observing the situation.
- When you are feeling confused and stressed about what's going on, do something physically active, such as walk, run, cook, rake leaves, shovel snow, dig in the garden, or build a fort.
- Try to be prepared at all times with things that will help distract you if you should become angry, such as an electronic device if you like listening to music. Make sure that the things you choose to help distract you are appropriate to the situation (for example, if your teacher doesn't allow devices, bring a book to class instead, provided you like to read).
- When lights, colors, smells, tastes, or sounds become overwhelming, find a way to speak up to help change the situation, or say that you want to leave the situation for a short time so that you can center yourself.

- If you have been bullied or picked on in the past and angry thoughts are getting stuck in your mind, use one of the calming exercises you have practiced, such as centering your attention on the soles of your feet and taking deep breaths. (If you are in the midst of being bullied, leave the situation immediately and seek the support of a caring adult.)

When you practice preventing meltdowns in the ways that you have worked on in this chapter, you are using your thoughts and feelings to build your independence. The more you practice, the stronger you will feel.

Chapter 9

your mind is the stage: get flexible and switch roles

When Ari has to go out and do something or be somewhere with other people, he feels anxious and uncomfortable, because he is very particular. He doesn't like eating certain foods, for example; if people drag him to a restaurant that doesn't have food he likes, he gets upset. He hates trying new things. People are always telling him that he needs to be more flexible—but he isn't even sure he knows what that means, except that he is supposed to do what somebody else wants instead of what he wants.

It is easier for Ari to just stay in his room by himself. He knows what is in there and doesn't have to deal with anybody else's ideas about what he should be doing. But his family doesn't understand why he spends so much time in his room. They don't realize that Ari feels best when he is alone in his room, where he feels most comfortable. Why don't they get it? he wonders.

You may find new situations stressful, even ones that are only a little different from ones you are already used to. You may feel unsure of what to do and how to behave in new situations, because you don't know what is expected of you.

Learning how to be flexible might help you feel less upset about dealing with change and more comfortable with new situations. Being flexible means being able to act differently in different situations. It does not mean changing who you are. You are always the same person, even if the situation you are in is new or different. It just means choosing to change how you act, to fit the situation.

If you have difficulty being flexible, you might not even realize when situations around you are changing. Noticing how a situation is changing is the first step in being flexible.

Being flexible means having choices. In different situations, you might discover that you don't need to change anything at all about how you would like to act. Or, you might find that making a small change, being flexible in a small way, will help you join in what other people are doing and have fun.

Being flexible isn't about saying yes to everything that everybody wants you to do. It is about being aware of what is happening in a changing situation and using your thoughts to make choices about how to act. Notice what's going on, notice your thoughts and feelings, and choose how to respond. *That* is flexibility.

In the following exercise, you will practice noticing how your thoughts are always changing. Your role in different situations changes, too. Different situations call for different roles. Your thoughts change as situations change. Noticing these changes in your own thoughts and feelings will help you discover how flexible you already are, and enhance your ability to choose different roles to play when you need to or want to.

This exercise teaches you to focus your attention and look at your own thoughts and how they change. As you practice noticing that your thoughts are changing all the time, remember that you are still the same person no matter what thoughts you are having. Even though your thoughts are always changing, you are still the same person who woke up this morning, went to school, played computer games at home, and had cheese popcorn for dessert, for example. Knowing this will help you remember that, later, while you are experimenting with playing different roles in different situations, you are still the same person too. You can choose to be flexible and act differently than you usually do, while still being in charge of who you are. The fact that your thoughts are already flexible and changing, but who you are as a person isn't, might be reassuring to you as you explore your own flexibility.

Give yourself two minutes for this exercise. Use a computer, a watch, a cell phone, or another device with a timer that you can set for two minutes. This exercise works best with your eyes closed, so that you can actually focus just on your thoughts and not on what's going on around you.

Exercise 9.1: Watching the Thought Show

Sit comfortably in your favorite place (for example, in your favorite chair, on your bed, or on the floor). Close your eyes, if you wish to.

Take three deep breaths, breathing out for longer than you breathe in. These longer out-breaths will help you feel relaxed in your body. Imagine that your mind is a quiet, still place with thoughts moving through it. Imagine that a show—a show of thoughts—is being performed on the stage of your mind, and you get to watch it.

Your goal in this exercise is only to watch your thoughts and enjoy the show, whatever the show turns out to be. Consider that because you are watching your thoughts, it stands to reason that your thoughts are something separate from you—otherwise, how could you sit back and observe them? In other words, you are not your thoughts. You are just you.

So, settle into your comfortable spot, get curious, and imagine that you are watching a show that you knew nothing about before you sat down. Your mind is like a stage for the show, so you don't have to go anywhere to watch it! Watch the thoughts as they come and go on the stage of your mind. Notice how each thought makes a brief appearance before another one comes along. The following questions can help you notice other things about your thoughts:

- Can you notice when a thought begins to appear on the stage of your mind?
- Can you see a thought end, as it leaves the stage of your mind?
- Is one thought replaced by another thought, or is it replaced by a crowd of other thoughts or even images?

- Do you ever notice a single thought, or are many thoughts on the stage of your mind all at the same time?
- Do the thoughts come in shapes, pictures, or both?
- Are the thoughts in the form of words?
- Are the thoughts in color, are they in black and white, or are they both?
- Are the thoughts a constantly changing mixture of shapes and words?

At the end of two minutes, your different thoughts will still be there, coming and going—changing all the time. You, the person watching the thought show, will still be the same person who started watching it. Let your thoughts carry on in the background as you shift your attention to the next activity.

The more you can notice about what's going on in your own thoughts, the more you will be able to choose what role might be best to play in different situations.

A *role* is simply the way that you act in relation to other people. Depending on what is happening and what relationship you have to the people in different situations, you need to play many different roles every day, such as student, family member, babysitter, and friend.

You might play some roles better than others, depending on what you notice or learn about what's going on, what you feel comfortable doing, what you find fun or interesting to try, or what you have practiced.

One way that you can notice and learn more about what roles you are playing in different situations, and also what roles other people are playing, is by paying attention to how people use their bodies. People's posture, body language, movements, gestures, and facial expressions send silent messages all the time about what they are thinking and feeling and the role that they are playing.

The way people act is influenced by their thoughts, just as the way you act is influenced by *your* thoughts. Watching people's bodies as they play their roles can help you imagine what thoughts they might be having.

By actively noticing how you and people around you are acting, and by paying attention to what people's faces and bodies are doing, you will know more about how to act in different situations. Later in this chapter are detailed examples of postures and facial expressions that might suggest specific roles.

In any situation, try to notice what thoughts or feelings you are having about what you are observing in others. You can use these thoughts to help you choose what role to play in the scene. You can decide to just listen to what people are saying, for example, or you can decide to add to a conversation.

In the following exercise, you will practice using *your* body to try on three different feelings (confident, annoyed, and excited) that you may see in others. This will help you recognize what people look like and how they act when they play different roles. You will also be practicing flexibility.

Exercise 9.2: Playing with the Feelings of Different Roles

Stand in front of a full-length mirror so that you can watch what you are doing with your body as if you were watching another person.

Confident. To begin to practice the role of a confident person, such as a boss or a leader, think confident thoughts, such as how great it is that you are in charge of deciding to do this exercise and how terrific you are at observing other people.

The body of a person in a confident role shows being in charge and knowing exactly what's going on. You can practice doing things with your body for this role that send signals of confidence. Standing in front of the mirror, focus on your body and do these things to show confidence:

1. Stand tall and straight, with your feet a little wider apart than usual. Keep your feet still and grounded by gravity.
2. Center your attention on your chest and expand your chest, pushing it out a little bit as you breathe in and out.
3. Relax your shoulders and make eye contact with yourself in the mirror, which makes you look and feel taller.
4. Breathe, and notice yourself just standing there, tall and strong in your body, with your feet flat on the floor.
5. Keep your mouth straight and your eyes calm. Don't smile and don't frown. Just look steadily into the mirror. This is a confident face.

6. Breathe and stay in this confident role for a few minutes. This is how a person who is in charge, feeling confidence, usually stands. Do you have a classmate or a family member who usually looks confident?

Annoyed. Now, you can practice being flexible by trying on a different role—one in which you are annoyed. When you are annoyed, you usually have grumpy, negative thoughts. These grumpy, negative thoughts influence how your face looks and how your posture looks. For just a moment (so that you don't become really annoyed), try this:

1. Think of something or someone that annoys you.

2. Clench your teeth or tighten your jaw.

3. Narrow your eyes into slits, as if you are looking through a mask.

4. Fold your arms tightly across the front of your body. This is how a person's face and body may look when the person is feeling annoyed. Think about someone you know who looks like this when he or she gets annoyed.

You have just played the role of an annoyed person. Don't stay in this role too long. You might want to stretch and breathe, shake out your arms, and open your mouth wide to help you get rid of the annoyed look.

Excited. Now that you've practiced the role of a confident person and played the role of an annoyed person, you can practice being flexible in trying out another role, the role of an excited person. When you are excited, you are usually happy and filled with energy. Use your thoughts to influence how your face and body look:

1. Think about something that you really like to do. You might notice that this thought makes you smile.

2. Let your smile grow a little bigger. You might notice little wrinkles forming near the outside edges of your eyes as you do so.

3. Let your arms, shoulders, and hands rise up. You might feel like jumping up and down. You might let yourself make an excited sound, such as "wow" or "yay!"

4. Breathe in and out, deeply and slowly. Let yourself enjoy just breathing and smiling and feeling excited.

This is how a person looks who is excited and happy. When someone looks like this and feels like this, he or she feels like sharing the excitement with others, or simply with another person. Sharing excited feelings with each other is something that friends do.

Here is a quick practice for switching roles. Keep looking in the mirror while you do this:

1. Imagine a situation where you would benefit from playing the role of a confident person, such as when you are giving a presentation in class. Shift your thoughts and your body language to those of a confident person.

2. Imagine a situation where something or someone is bothering you so that you can try on the role of an annoyed person. Shift your thoughts and your posture to those of an annoyed person. (In real life, it would be good for you to notice that your thoughts and body posture are sending you the message that you are annoyed in this type of situ-

ation. This way, you will have a choice of asking for what you want or walking away from the situation, so that your annoyance doesn't grow into strong anger.)

3. Imagine that you want to listen openly to the ideas of others or that you want to be a friend to someone. Shift your thoughts and your body language to play the role of a person who is happy and excited to share and listen to ideas.

Now you have a sense of what it is like to play different roles in different situations. What other feelings can you think of that would help you play different roles? Try them out in the mirror if you like.

When you practice and experiment with different roles, you are being flexible in the way you use your body and your thoughts.

Another way you can acquire a sense for how people communicate using their bodies is to watch a TV show or movie with live actors (not animation). As you watch, pay close attention to how the people on the screen move and the postures they take. Notice their facial expressions. Notice the thoughts you might be having about what you see. What do these things tell you about their different roles? When you watch someone telling other people what to do, what signals is that person sending that show he or she is feeling confident? When someone says something that lets you know he or she is annoyed, what can you notice about his or her facial expression or his or her posture? When you watch someone who is happily going along with another person's ideas, pay attention to how his or her face and posture send the signal that he or she is relaxed, comfortable, and excited.

Experiencing how different roles feel in your body and noticing how your thoughts help you assume different roles when you want to do so will help build your skill at being an independent person. You will be building the freedom to choose to be flexible as you grow, rather than being stuck not being able to cope with change.

Chapter 10

makeover magic: improve your self-esteem

Mia feels "down" most of the time. She doesn't feel very good about herself. She thinks about what is wrong with her all the time. She never thinks good things about herself. She doesn't have much confidence.

Even when Mia is good at something, she tells herself that she isn't good enough. She is a good writer, but she tells herself that no one would want to read what she writes. Even when people tell her that her writing is good, she doesn't believe them. She stays stuck in a negative view of herself. Her negative view of herself makes her feel bad most of the time. Feeling that she isn't as good as other people makes her worry about whether she will ever be able to find something she is good enough at to earn a living.

How you view yourself is called your "self-esteem." It is common for teenagers to feel a bit awkward and uncomfortable much of the time, and to feel as if they don't fit in with those around them. If this is how you feel, you aren't the only one. Many teenagers don't feel very good about themselves. This is known as having low self-esteem.

As a teenager, it is very helpful to learn to build up your self-esteem in a positive way. This is even more important for teenagers with autism, who find it especially difficult to fit in with others.

The exercises in this chapter will show you ways to feel good about yourself and help you think of yourself in a positive way. Through practice, you can learn to say things silently to yourself that will improve your self-esteem, reduce your stress, and help you build up a feeling of independence. When you feel better about yourself, you will be more able to rely on yourself, which automatically makes you more independent.

The first step in improving your self-esteem is to listen to your thoughts about yourself and notice how many of them are negative. *Negative thoughts* are thoughts that are critical, either of someone (*He is boring*) or something in the world (*I hate school*) or of yourself (*I'm stupid*). When you stop to notice your thoughts, you might be surprised at how many of them are negative. However, it is normal for teenagers and people of all ages to have many negative thoughts. It just seems to be part of how our minds work.

You might notice that many of your negative thoughts are self-critical thoughts, such as the following:

- *I can't do that.*
- *I am not the kind of person who can do that.*
- *Nobody likes me or cares about me.*
- *People already don't like me, so why bother?*
- *I don't fit in.*
- *I will never fit in.*
- *Nobody wants to be my friend.*
- *I will never have any friends.*
- *Things never turn out right for me.*

The following exercise will teach you to notice your thoughts without judgment. This might be hard to do. It will take a certain amount of courage, because you will be taking time to listen to your negative thoughts about yourself, which might not feel very good. You might be tempted to try to push certain thoughts out of your mind and hold on to others. However, it is important that you listen to each thought without trying to change it. You don't need to try to figure out whether these are good or bad thoughts or even whether they mean anything about you. The goal is just to listen to your thoughts and notice which ones are negative. Then, in another exercise, you will learn how to do something positive to change your thoughts. Making this positive change is the "makeover magic."

Exercise 10.1: Noticing Your Thoughts Without Judgment

Sit in a quiet place where you can be comfortable and relaxed. Close your eyes, if you wish to. (This exercise is easiest to do with your eyes closed, so that you aren't distracted by anything going on around you.)

Imagine that your mind is a stage, and focus your attention on your many thoughts as they come and go across the stage of your mind.

Notice that some thoughts are positive thoughts (for example, if you think, ***This is easy for me***) and some thoughts are negative or self-judging, critical thoughts (for example, if you think, ***This is a stupid exercise—I can't do this***). Try noticing your thoughts with curiosity to see how many of them might be negative or judgmental.

Just notice all of your thoughts without adding extra judgments on top of them. Try letting each thought that comes to your mind just be there for a while, until it goes and is replaced by another one. This is what "accepting" your thoughts means. All thoughts simply come and go.

As you notice so many thoughts coming and going, you can let the different kinds, positive and negative, come into your mind and watch them go. You can accept them without deciding anything about them, including whether they are true or false.

Thoughts are just thoughts. They will come and go. Each time you notice a thought, you can say to yourself "thought" or "thinking." This way of naming a thought is a way of noticing it and letting it go. You don't have to believe the thought or hold on to it. Just notice it. Notice how thoughts come and go.

We have taught this thought-watching exercise to both teenagers and adults, and all people who do it discover that they have many more negative thoughts than positive thoughts. It just seems to be a part of how the human mind works. All people have negative thoughts about themselves, too. What makes a difference in people's self-esteem is how they react to all of these negative opinions about themselves.

After you have practiced noticing how thoughts come and go, you can practice paying particular attention to any negative thought once you notice it.

When you notice a negative thought while it is happening, you can label that thought by calling it a "negative thought." Labeling a thought a "negative thought" is not the same as a judgment. It is just a way of noting the kind of thought that it is. Don't worry about having negative thoughts—as we said, everyone has them. It is normal for humans to have negative thoughts. When you "worry" about having negative thoughts, this means you are actually judging them, so don't "worry"!

Labeling a thought gives you control over it. Once you label a negative thought, you can change it, if you choose to do so. You can give the thought a makeover. The next exercise will show you how.

Can you imagine what it would be like to think better thoughts about yourself? What if Mia (from the beginning of the chapter) told herself that she was a good writer? And what if she believed it?

Some negative thoughts create anxiety and stress because they are pessimistic about the future. Imagine yourself facing a situation in which you usually tell yourself how awful you are and how badly it will turn out. You can call these thoughts "negative predictions." These thoughts try to convince you that you can tell the future and that the future will be bad. In addition to noticing and labeling negative thoughts about yourself, you will practice noticing and labeling negative predictions about the future. You can give these a makeover too.

The way you work "makeover magic" on your negative thoughts and negative predictions is by changing the stressful words of a negative thought to words that can make you feel better and less stressed.

Here is an example of using makeover magic to change a thought: You notice yourself thinking, *I am just stupid in history class—I can't do this essay*. This is actually a two-part thought! The thought is a negative one about yourself (*I am stupid*) and also makes a negative prediction (*I can't do this*). So, you say to yourself "negative thought" and "negative prediction," and then you respond, *I am not stupid—I am curious, and I can try writing this essay*.

Any time you feel as if you don't know a lot about something, remind yourself that you can get curious and learn more. This is more accurate and is more helpful than just calling yourself stupid. Practice saying this positive thought silently to yourself several times. Now, practice out loud. By practicing out loud, you get to hear your own voice, which makes the makeover feel more real. Here is how it might sound: *I can get curious and learn more. [repeat] I can get curious and learn more.*

Here is another thought makeover example: You catch yourself thinking, *No one will sit with me at lunch*. You label this thought as a negative prediction, reminding yourself that you can't really tell the future. A negative prediction is not a fact. You don't have to believe it. You don't know that no one will sit with you at lunch, or even where you will sit at lunch yet. You can notice your negative prediction and then approach the future with curiosity instead: *I wonder where I will choose to sit at lunch?*

Here is another example of a thought in need of a makeover: *I am weird, and no one likes me*. This thought is negative about yourself (*I am weird*), and it also makes a negative assumption about the way other people feel about you (*No one likes me*), which could lead to negative predictions such as that no one would ever want to get to know you. What happens when you get curious about how you can turn this into a positive thought and a positive prediction? You might come up with *I'm different. Someone might want to get to know me.*

Exercise 10.2: Giving Your Negative Thoughts a Makeover

For each of the following examples of thoughts that need makeovers, try saying the negative thought out loud. Then, say the makeover words, which point to a more realistic and logical way to view the situation, out loud. Saying the makeover words three times gives you extra practice with the new thought. Even though the makeover words may not sound right to you, or may not come easily to you, saying them out loud will be very helpful as you practice giving negative thoughts makeovers. The more you practice giving even these example thoughts makeovers, the more you will feel in charge of your own thoughts. The magic of the makeover is in your decision to try doing it.

- Example: ***I am a terrible writer.***

  Makeover: *I am learning how to write better. I am learning how to write better. I am learning how to write better.*

- Example: ***I am not the kind of person who gets invited to parties.***

  Makeover: *I am a person who is good at deejaying family parties; maybe people would invite me to parties if they knew that. I am a person who is good at deejaying family parties; maybe people would invite me to parties if they knew that. I am a person who is good at deejaying family parties; maybe people would invite me to parties if they knew that.*

- Example: ***I am terrible at games; I can never figure out what's going on.***

  Makeover: *If I don't know what's going on, I can ask somebody who knows, and that person can help me figure it out. If I don't know what's going on, I can ask somebody who knows, and that person can help me figure it out. If I don't know what's going on, I can ask somebody who knows, and that person can help me figure it out.*

- Example: ***I am terrible at sports, and people hate having me on their team.***

  Makeover: *I am not so good at sports, but I am really good at computer games, and people like to play them with me. I am not so good at sports, but I am really good at computer games, and people like to play them with me. I am not so good at sports, but I am really good at computer games, and people like to play them with me.*

What did you notice about your reactions as you tried these makeovers? Were you judging yourself? Or were you patient with yourself as you tried something new? You might have felt doubtful at first and then noticed that you actually felt a little better as you played with this idea of making over a thought.

The final step in this exercise is for you to move from these examples you have practiced to one of your own negative thoughts. Don't judge the thought; just notice it and decide whether you want to give it a makeover. You can notice the thought and just choose to let it go. Or, you can notice the thought and decide to give it a makeover. If you do choose to give it a makeover, then make up a sentence that changes the thought to words that make you feel more confident. Say that new sentence out loud at least three times.

When Mia (from the beginning of the chapter) practiced making over her thought that she wasn't a good enough writer and that no one would want to read her writing, she began to feel much better about herself and less stressed about her writing. Here are the makeover words that she created for herself: *I kind of like writing, and I am learning how to write better.*

As you practice your own thought makeovers, see which words feel most comfortable for you and look for opportunities to try applying makeover magic in different situations, both in and outside of school. The more you try it, the better you will get at it and the more confident you will start to feel.

Part III

Reach Out to Connect with Others and Direct Your Life

Chapter 11

play the role of a scientist: get curious

Anthony dreads lunch. Lunch means standing in line. Lunch means being jostled by crowds of other students finding places to sit. Lunch means constant noise bouncing off echoing surfaces. Lunch means feeling disoriented and confused by not being able to understand the voices coming from every direction.

The pushy crowds, noise, and confusion make Anthony feel completely overwhelmed. So he tries to hide inside himself until lunchtime is over. He tries to escape by looking down, not making eye contact with anyone around him, and sitting by himself in a corner as far away from other people as possible. He eats just a little so that he can get out of the lunchroom fast. Then, he finds a quiet place to sit where no one can see him until it is time for his next class. Sometimes he feels lonely as a result of this avoidance, but he doesn't know any other way to cope with the confusion of lunchtime.

We human beings are mammals. All mammals are naturally curious about their environment. Curiosity is a built-in survival tool. Being curious helps us learn what is safe and what is dangerous, where to find food, which creatures are good companions, and which creatures are not trustworthy. Curiosity empowers us.

Anthony may not realize it, but hiding inside himself isn't the most useful solution to his misery when he feels overwhelmed by what's going on around him. In a way, he needs to do the exact opposite of hiding in order to feel less stressed and overwhelmed. Instead of focusing more inside himself, he needs to get curious about what is actually going on outside of him. If Anthony can get curious, then he won't be so confused. (But he should start by practicing curiosity in a less stressful, less confusing place than the lunchroom, such as his own room.)

Think of the times when you feel a bit like Anthony—overwhelmed and confused by crowds or by too many sights and sounds so that you just want to hide. Everyone feels this way sometimes. When you feel like this, if you can look for things to get curious about, you can have more information and, as a result, experience less confusion. When you experience less confusion, you will be less stressed about being around other people in everyday situations. When you are less stressed about being around other people, it will become easier to connect with them, if you want to.

Try out the exercises in this chapter to increase your curiosity, which will decrease your confusion and stress, especially when you need to be around other people.

The following exercise asks you to practice observing yourself and your world with curiosity. You will be preparing your scientific mind to notice what's going on. You will begin in the privacy of your own room and then move outdoors to practice. Remember, there is always something to observe, wherever you are.

Exercise 11.1: Be Curious—Ask Yourself, "What's Going On?"

Begin by standing or sitting still and notice the sensations of breathing in your body, while keeping your eyes open. This will help you calm yourself and be ready to observe.

Now, look around the room with curiosity. Try to find something in the room that you never noticed before. Check the walls, the ceiling, the floor, and the furniture. You are gathering information about what is in this room. Gather this information without any judgment. You are just looking with curiosity. Try to look at everything in the room as if you have never seen it before.

Next, walk outside your room. Go into another room or go outside of your house through the front door or back door. Then, just stop and look around with curiosity.

1. Begin by looking and listening right in front of you. Be curious—what colors do you see? What objects do you see? Be curious—what sounds can you hear? Try to look at everything in front of you without judging anything.
2. Turn your head to the right. Now, what do you see? What do you hear? How are these sights and sounds different from what you saw and heard a moment ago?

3. Turn your head to the left. What do you see? What do you hear? What is different from the sights and sounds you just noticed a moment ago?

You are training your mind to use your natural curiosity—like a scientist or a secret agent. Curiosity can help you see, hear, and figure out what's going on!

If you practice this exercise several times a day, you will quickly build your natural ability to be curious and bring back information to your home base. You can think of this as building up your curiosity muscle so that you can use the strength of your curiosity when you want to reduce your stress.

Having just practiced using your curiosity indoors and outdoors, you are ready to practice using your curiosity in a more complicated and busy environment, such as your school. Your school is filled with many, many people. You can think of these people as other "curious creatures" like yourself.

You might feel anxious or awkward or shy around kids at school, so try to find and direct your own curiosity. You can use what you have learned to focus your curiosity away from your own shyness. When you are with other people, you can practice gently shifting your focus away from yourself and toward what's going on outside of you. Just by focusing your curiosity on others, without doing anything else, you are reaching out. You are connecting with other people simply by paying attention to them.

Curiosity can help you understand situations at school. Curiosity can also help you make decisions about whether you want to get to know someone, enter a group, or join a conversation. Curiosity allows us to notice things we wouldn't see otherwise.

Simply seeing what's going on, without deciding whether it is good or bad, can have a relaxing, calming effect. It might not feel easy for you to use your natural curiosity at first, but the more you practice being curious, the easier it will become. You will probably find that it is more interesting to learn about the world around you than to retreat inside yourself.

In the following exercise, you will be thinking about a confusing social scene at school and using your imagination to see it as a scientist or a secret agent on a mission might see it. You will be taking your curiosity to school and practicing it right there. Then, you can use your imagination to play with transforming what you see at school into social scenes that are simpler and easier to understand.

Exercise 11.2: Curiosity Goes to School

First, close your eyes and center yourself by focusing on your breathing. When you feel calm, imagine yourself going to school in the role of a scientist or a secret agent, using your natural curiosity to gather information about the behavior of your fellow creatures. You won't be judging what you see; you will just be gathering information. Does this seem like a very different role for you to play than usual? It probably is. So, be sure to try to imagine this nonjudgmental, information-gathering role as clearly as you can:

1. See yourself walking into your school and noticing everything about the building.

2. See yourself noticing a group of people standing together and talking. Notice what they are wearing, how they are talking, and how they are moving.

3. Do all your observing without judging the people. Imagine that you haven't yet made a decision to try to join them. You are simply observing, taking in all the information. If you are imagining yourself in the role of a secret agent, think about what you would write down in your intelligence report.

You can do this in your imagination as often as you wish, to prepare for using your curiosity in real life.

Then, practice taking your curiosity with you when you actually go to school:

1. When you walk toward your school, take a moment to notice the outside and then the inside of the building as you walk in.

2. Notice something going on among a few people who are talking together. Try to observe what's going on by getting curious.

3. Pause, and focus on your breathing for a moment to stay calm. You don't have to do anything else. Just observe and stay curious. See what you can learn.

    - *Is one person moving more than the others?*

    - *Are these people's voices loud or soft?*

- *Are these people talking quickly or slowly?*
- *Are these people looking at each other, or are they all looking at something else?*
- *What do you think these people might be feeling or thinking, from the expressions on their faces?*

4. Decide whether you want to go up to that small group to talk with them. It is your choice. Now that you have used your curiosity to observe all the details, you can direct yourself to reach out and connect, or you can choose not to connect right now.

When you get home, you might want to write down your observations—what you tried out and what happened—in a log to keep track of your findings.

Some people with autism find it easier to understand animals than to understand people. They might even like being around animals more than being around people. This might be true for you, or you might have a talent for relating to and understanding animals. The next exercise might sound kind of silly at first. It is something very different.

Exercise 11.3: Friendly Animals

Just for fun, watch a group of kids at school, noticing how they talk and move. Consider how they might remind you of different animals.

- Does anyone's behavior (way of walking, talking, moving) remind you of how a tall, graceful giraffe moves and looks?
- Does the way someone looks or acts make you think of a massive bear?
- Does anyone seem to be like a tiny, quiet mouse?

If what you see strikes you as funny, don't laugh out loud at people while you are looking at them. Just notice and let yourself laugh on the inside while you continue observing. This can be a fun way to help you relax around people. So, go ahead and try becoming very interested and curious as you observe your surroundings and people at school.

Try the next exercise when you want to connect with other people at school while practicing your curiosity.

Exercise 11.4: Natural Curiosity

Find two or more kids hanging out together whom you know and might want to join. Take a deep breath, and just watch them for a short time. Use your curiosity to observe. Don't stare. Just notice and take in what you see. You are doing a scientific investigation, checking things out before moving ahead so that you know what's going on. You are looking over a situation before jumping into it or running away from it. You are developing skill and interest in being curious about others.

When you feel that you have learned enough to have an idea about what's going on, approach the kids and try saying hello. See what happens when you reach out to connect. Stay in the role of curious scientist or secret agent, watching what happens. You can be curious as you notice what's going on inside of you, and you can be curious as you notice how the kids are responding to you. Ask yourself whether you have learned anything new about these kids. Taking a moment to see what you have learned will help you take the next action step. Consider writing it down at home. Stay curious about what your next action will be.

Continue practicing your natural curiosity everywhere you go. The more you practice, the more you will know what's going on around you.

When Anthony (from the beginning of the chapter) learned that he could use his natural curiosity, he practiced being curious as much as he could in every situation, including in the lunchroom. When he was in this role, he felt less stressed and less confused at lunchtime. He was even able to try joining a group of kids eating at one of the tables.

Like Anthony, the more you practice using your curiosity, the more you will learn about what's going on around you and the less stressed you will feel in any situation. You will find that being around others gives you a lot to be curious about and that your curiosity helps you connect with other people as you focus on gathering information instead of hiding inside yourself. You will be better able to direct your life when it comes to choosing between being alone and reaching out to others.

Chapter 12

you are the director: advocate for yourself

Emily is bothered by a great many things. She is bothered by people telling her lots of things to do all at once, instead of just one thing at a time. She is bothered by loud sounds and bright red colors. She is bothered by people standing too close to her. When someone walks by her and brushes against her even slightly, she feels like jumping straight up into the air and screaming. She hates it when a teacher or one of her family members gives her a pat on the shoulder. She especially doesn't like people trying to hug her. She sometimes even pushes them away. People often tell her that they are just trying to be nice and that she is being rude and unfriendly.

Emily really needs a good way to let people know when she is bothered by something. She needs to be able to make people understand that she would *like* to be friendly, but that she can't stand certain kinds of touching and other things that don't seem to bother most people.

Like Emily, you might be bothered by a lot of different things. It is actually pretty common for teens with autism to have strong reactions to being touched very lightly or to being poked or tickled. Low buzzing sounds that other people might not notice at all may be hugely irritating to you. Some colors or lights may be just too bright for your eyes. You might be easily annoyed by many things you can't avoid in your school day, such as the sounds of pencil sharpeners, the hum or flicker of fluorescent lights, the textures and smells of cafeteria food, and all those people crowding you or bumping into you. You probably understand just how Emily feels.

The exercises in this chapter will give you practice in paying attention to exactly what is bothering you and taking a moment to talk to yourself about it, instead of only feeling annoyed. Then, after you talk to yourself, you can actively speak up to someone else about it. This is called "advocating for" (watching out for and sticking up for) yourself.

Start by making a list right now of some of the things that annoy you most at school or at home. In this chapter, you will practice talking to yourself about being annoyed. Then, you will practice taking action about the specific things that are bothering you.

There is a big difference between being annoyed and *actually noticing* that you are annoyed. The following exercise will teach you an action plan for noticing that you are annoyed and changing what you say to yourself (your "self-talk") and what you do (your "script") when you are annoyed. Instead of following what might be your usual script (keeping quiet, staying frustrated, or getting angry), you can choose to create a different script. Changing your script can help you be calmer and less annoyed, and take charge of your situation.

Exercise 12.1: Changing the Script

At any time during your day when you think you might be annoyed, check in with your body. Check different places in your body:

- Is your jaw clenched?
- Is your face frowning?
- Do your legs feel jittery or like running away?
- Are you making fists?
- Are your arms folded tight against your chest?

Often, your body can tell you that you are annoyed before your mind can. If you notice that you are annoyed, know that you ***have a right to be annoyed!*** This is different from being angry that other people don't know what is bothering you. You have a right to your own feelings, including annoyance. So, say to yourself, "I am annoyed," and feel how true that is. Then, use the following script to help yourself calm down and figure out what exactly is annoying you:

1. Say to yourself, "I am really annoyed with..." (name the specific thing or behavior that you are annoyed with, referring to the list you created in this chapter if necessary).

2. Take a deep breath in, and let a very, very long breath out.

3. Repeat steps 1 and 2 at least three times, until you begin to notice some relaxation in your body.

This is a positive first step in being able to direct yourself. When you notice that your body and your mind are starting to feel calm, then you are ready to take action.

Now that you have practiced noticing the feeling of being annoyed, you are ready to rehearse some action steps to help you advocate for yourself. In the next exercise, you will practice directing yourself to do something that will help you change the annoying situation.

You probably already know what you *don't* want in an annoying situation. It is helpful to practice thinking about and saying what you *do* want. Once you are able to focus on what you do want, you will need to think about how to ask for what you want in a way that will make it easy for other people to say yes!

Try this exercise when you are annoyed, after doing the previous exercise.

Exercise 12.2: Directing Yourself

After you realize that you are annoyed, just follow this basic script:

1. State the problem out loud to a person who can help you, such as your adviser, a teacher, or a friend.
2. Explain what the problem is and why it is bothering you.
3. Suggest a solution that gets you what you want or need.
4. Thank the person in advance for helping you.

You can customize this script to use with people in all kinds of situations. Each time you try out a new version of this script, you are learning that you can direct yourself and that you have choices.

Here are three examples:

- You are aware that the buzzing sound of a heater is bothering you in class. You say to yourself: "I am annoyed by the sound of that heater buzzing. I have a problem with the sound, so I need to sit in a place far enough away so that I am not constantly hearing it." Then, you say to your teacher: "The buzzing sound of the heater is getting on my nerves. It would help me do my work if I move to another seat, away from the heater. Thanks if you can suggest another seat."
- Your classmate is tapping a pencil on the table while you are working in class, and you can feel it starting to make you mad. You say to your classmate: "It would help me if you'd please stop tapping your pencil like that. It's making it kind of hard for me to concentrate. Thanks!"

- You are going to eat lunch with a friend at school, but you don't like how crowded the lunchroom looks. You say to your friend: "This table looks so crowded. Would it be okay if we sit where there aren't so many people? I would feel so much better. Thanks."

Now, make up other scripts to practice that have to do with things you have already learned really bother you. It helps if you write these scripts down. Writing something down helps your brain remember it when you need to. For example, Emily (from the beginning of the chapter) could create a script that says, "I would like to talk with you, but I don't like it when you touch my shoulder."

When you prepare scripts like this, you'll have them ready in case you need them in annoying situations. Not only do you have a right to feel annoyed, you have a right to do something about it!

The feeling of annoyance gives you very useful information about what you need to help you feel more comfortable. Your new scripts will give you ways to help yourself get what you need. And, they will give you some ideas about what to say to other people so that you are advocating for yourself.

Chapter 13

the positive channel: build your health and happiness

Everyone thinks Mike always looks sad, cranky, or down. In fact, he usually does feel down. He is always remembering things that went wrong or figuring out what might go wrong next. He is trying to avoid trouble by thinking about how to stop bad things from happening. Or, he is thinking about how something isn't going to work out, so that he doesn't set himself up for disappointment by having high expectations. To him, this seems like a smart thing to do and a good way to go through life.

The only problem is that Mike forgets about the good stuff that has happened. Even if he notices something good when it happens, he doesn't remember it, because he doesn't focus on it. Since it has already happened, he figures that it is over and he doesn't have to worry about it anymore. He needs to focus on his next worry. He doesn't even consider the possibility that he could get anything more out of a good experience by recalling it.

Your brain, just like everyone's brain, is naturally wired to keep track of bad experiences. Your brain keeps track of bad experiences to try to protect you by reminding you of things that you should avoid and watch out for. This natural impulse to focus on possible threats helped early humans hunt or scavenge for food in the midst of dangerous predators. You can imagine your brain as being set to a negative channel most of the time. This negative channel is useful when it comes to surviving in dangerous situations, but it is not that useful in building health and happiness in your everyday life. Focusing on bad experiences gets in the way of trying new things, such as going to a new place or meeting new friends.

If your brain is always keeping track of bad things, who is going to keep track of the good things so that you can try to include more of them in your life? You are! You are in charge of keeping track of the good things, by deliberately switching your brain to a positive channel.

Only you can switch your brain to a positive channel when you are feeling down. Other people may try, however, by telling you to "Cheer up" or "Have a nice day," for example. Sometimes this can be annoying. These people are trying to be helpful, but they don't quite get it: only *you* can change the channel that your brain is tuned to.

You can switch your brain to a positive channel simply by thinking about something good that has happened to you each day. This is more than practicing a natural ability—it is a skill you need to work on, something you need to get better at doing on purpose. You can remember or think about some really small, positive thing that happened in your day. What counts is that you liked it, or it felt good, or it mattered to you. Here are a few examples of things you could notice in order to switch your brain to a positive channel:

- You liked the way your hair looked this morning.
- You were able to find a really sharp pencil to use for the math test.
- You remembered to put your homework in your book bag.
- Your favorite show is on tonight.

Do you have some ideas about the types of things that would be on your favorite positive channel? The following exercise will help you practice paying attention to even the tiniest positive parts of your day.

Exercise 13.1: Focusing on the Positive

Start by sitting or standing still, either in your room or outside where you won't be bothered. Keep your eyes open, because you will be using them. Center yourself in your body by taking several deep breaths. Then, look around you and notice anything that could make you smile or that you simply like.

- If you are in your room, notice anything in your room that you like—big or small—such as the pile of rumpled clothes on the floor, your cell phone, a picture of your dog on the beach, your battery collection, or your bass guitar.

- If you are outside, look for any part of your surroundings that you like, such as a bright yellow dandelion popping up in the middle of a yard, a puddle on the sidewalk, squirrels chasing each other up a tree, a cement mixer, or soft gray clouds filling the sky.

Take a moment to practice this exercise every day when you first wake up, and again when you walk outside of your house. Notice how this practice affects how you feel, first when you are by yourself and then when you are around other people.

You can make notes every day about what makes you feel happy or what makes you smile. You will notice that some of the things that make you feel happy or smile are the same from day to day, and some things are different. Keeping a notebook of positive things that you notice can be fun and actually helps you notice even more positive things about your day.

At the end of your day, you can ask yourself, "What went well today?" Usually our minds focus on what went wrong or what we didn't like. So, teaching your mind to focus on what went well, what made you smile, or what gave you some happy feelings is a way to build up a strong positive channel in your mind. This positive channel is very good for your health. Recent research shows that positive thinking is good for your body, as well as for your mind.

Now that you have been trying out a positive channel and paying attention to how it affects you, you will try switching to a positive channel when you notice that you are feeling down. This might be a bit difficult, because it is very normal for anyone who is feeling down not to actually notice that feeling. It is worth trying to notice feeling down, because it affects how you see things and what you do, even if you aren't completely aware of it. When you can notice that you are feeling down, you have a chance to change the channel. The next exercise teaches you several easy ways to notice when you are feeling down, by focusing your attention on your body and your mind.

Exercise 13.2: Changing the Channel When You Are Feeling Down

First, focus your attention on your body and see whether your body is feeling low in energy. This isn't the same as being tired or sleepy. When your body feels as if it doesn't have much energy, you just don't feel like doing anything. Then, focus your attention on your thoughts and see whether your mind is creating negative thoughts. These might include thoughts about how things are going to be bad in the future or thoughts about bad things that have happened in the past. Low energy in your body and thoughts about what might or did go wrong are signs that your brain is tuned to a negative channel.

The way that you can switch your brain to a positive channel, if you want, is to start thinking about things that you like, things that make you happy, or things that are fun for you to do. If you catch yourself feeling low, you can decide to switch to a channel that has a memory of a good thing that happened in the past. You could try checking out a channel about a good thing in the future—something you are looking forward to. You could switch to a channel about something about your day so far that you liked or that worked for you.

You can practice doing this for fun, even if you don't feel very low, just to see whether you can do it. This is like when you were practicing focusing on the positive while sitting or standing still, but now you are doing it while you are going about your day. Any time that you catch your brain stuck on a negative channel, just stop and say to yourself, "I am choosing now to switch to a positive channel." When you practice switching channels like this, you are also practicing directing your own life. Go on with your day and enjoy your positive thoughts!

Now that you have practiced noticing the kinds of things that you can use to create a positive channel, you can actually design specific channels to turn to. This next exercise is designed to help you keep track of things you like—things that you consider to be positive. You can turn to these positive channels as easily as you can change the TV channel with a remote control.

Exercise 13.3: Designing Positive Channels

Many teens with autism are really good at making collections of all sorts of things that they have a particular interest in. If you have a talent for collecting, you can use it to help you design a positive channel that is especially powerful.

For example:

- If you are excited about seeing movies, you could create a list of movie titles or the directors or actors in the movies that you have really liked. Then, you can switch to that positive channel of movie information any time that you want to make yourself feel a bit happier. You can name this your "movie channel."

- If you are fascinated by numbers, you could have some reminder of an interesting formula handy and turn to that as a positive channel-changer. You could even keep a little notebook of formulas to use when you want to think about them because that makes you feel good. You can name this your "numbers channel."
- If you have a specific interest, such as trains, fossils, or video games, you can design channels for each of your special interests so that you can turn to them in your mind whenever you want to.

These collections of things you like, things that make you feel happy even for a moment, are great for building the power of your positive channel. Practicing looking through your collection of things that you noticed during the day, or things that you are looking forward to in the future, will help you get used to switching to a positive channel as a regular part of your everyday life.

Once you have practiced creating collections of things you like for your positive channels, you can keep noticing more things that you like and add these things to your positive collections. Because you will be actively looking for what you want to have on your positive channel, you will be actively building your own health and happiness.

By paying attention to small positive things or positive experiences that you can add to your collection, you might find that you look forward to switching to your positive channels. Your positive channels might turn out to be more fun than you expected.

Chapter 14

practice kindness: make friends

Whenever James is repairing electronics, he feels very focused and peaceful. He enjoys working with machines, and he is good at it. People in his family and some kids at school often bring him things that don't work, such as watches, computers, and cell phones. He is good at fixing things and telling people what to do to make something work.

James wonders whether he might ever feel as peaceful when he is having dinner with his family or hanging out with kids at school as when he is repairing electronics. But he doesn't think he is very good at knowing what to do around people. He can't figure out what makes it so easy for other people to fit in and so hard for him. He wishes he could connect with people the way he connects wires in electronics! He feels as though all he knows how to do is fix things for other people or show them how to make things work. He wishes he knew how to make friends and have fun hanging out and doing things with them.

If you are interested in making more connections with people, you are probably ready to try some ways of reaching out that will help you develop relationships with others. In this chapter, you will learn some specific ways to make friends and keep friends.

One way to reach out to make friends and keep friends is to practice a specific skill called "kindness." You might not have ever thought of kindness as an actual skill, but it is. Learning how to be kind requires just as much focus, concentration, and effort as learning to ride a bike or learning to play the guitar. Just like other skills that are easy for some and challenging for others to learn, kindness may be hard or easy for you to master. But kindness is very helpful when it comes to making friends, so it is worth giving it a try.

Practicing kindness can help you become calm and peaceful, which can make it easier to do the mindfulness work that will help you calm yourself, build independence, and connect with others. What is especially powerful about the skill of kindness is that it also gives you a specific way of reaching out to others.

By having you practice kindness, on purpose, the exercises in this chapter will teach you a very different way to be with yourself and with others than the way you are probably used to. The practice of kindness begins with being kind to yourself. Being kind to yourself helps you be more patient, understanding, and accepting toward yourself. Practicing kindness toward yourself will give you more patience, peace, and calm. *Compassion* is a feeling of caring for yourself and others. All humans are born with the ability to feel compassion, which originates in a certain part of the brain. By practicing kindness toward yourself, you can increase your brain's ability to feel compassion.

One way to practice kindness toward yourself is by thinking positive wishes for yourself. You can do this by thinking positive thoughts about yourself and about the sort of person you would like to be. You can think about the positive qualities that you want to develop in yourself.

When you think of wishes for yourself, you can "send" these wishes to yourself by saying short sentences silently to yourself. This is called "setting an intention." An intention is a deliberate choice to do something or act in a certain way. By setting an intention through a wish for yourself, you can help your good qualities grow. One way to begin your sentences when you send wishes to yourself is to use the words "May I be" or "May I have." Here are some examples:

- If you wish to be calm, you could say, "May I be calm."
- If you wish to be strong, you could say, "May I be strong."
- If you wish to be more kind, you could say, "May I be kind to myself and to others."
- If you wish to feel peaceful, you could say, "May I feel peaceful."
- If you wish to feel comfortable with other people, you could say, "May I be comfortable with others."

Before you practice extending kindness to others, the following exercise will help you show kindness to yourself.

Exercise 14.1: Practicing Kindness Toward Yourself

Just try saying some of these sentences silently to yourself every day for a week, and see what happens.

- *"May I be calm."*
- *"May I be strong."*
- *"May I be kind to myself and to others."*
- *"May I feel peaceful."*
- *"May I be comfortable with others."*

Being kind to yourself by saying positive wishes isn't like wishing for magic. It isn't about wishing for specific things you want for yourself, such as a new bike. It isn't about getting your way. It is about setting an intention to be a certain kind of person.

Think about the kind of person that you want to be. What qualities would make you that kind of person? We all have some ability to be calm, strong, confident, kind, patient, loving, caring, healthy, brave, and happy. Choose two or three qualities that are important to you and would help you be the kind of person you want to be. Then, put these qualities into sentences and send these good wishes to yourself. For example:

- *"May I grow into a more confident person."*
- *"May I grow into a happier person."*
- *"May I become a more patient person."*

Any time when you have a few minutes to yourself—for example, when you are sitting down to do some homework, when you are walking, or when you are riding in a car, on a train, or on a bus—you can relax, breathe, and say your chosen sentences over and over in your mind.

When you are comfortable with this practice of giving kindness to yourself, you can also send positive wishes silently to someone else. You have practiced becoming a better friend to yourself; in the next two exercises, you can practice becoming a better friend to others. Extending kindness to others helps you feel even better about yourself and better about other people. Not only will this make you feel more open to connecting with others, it will make it easier for others to connect with you.

Exercise 14.2: Sending Kindness to Others

Imagine someone you care about, such as a friend, a cousin, a favorite teacher, a lab partner, or a parent. Try to picture that person in your mind, and think about sending him or her good wishes or wishing him or her well in some way you think he or she would like. Put this good wish into a sentence. For example:

- I hope you have a great bike ride.
- I hope that you are able to get that computer program to run correctly.
- I hope that you get to play basketball after work.
- I hope that you can come to the camp reunion.

The positive wish can be anything—what is important is that you think about someone specific and come up with a specific wish for that person. Then, when the wish is clear in your mind, say it to yourself, imagining that you are saying it to that person. In this way, you are thinking about what other people might care about, and you are practicing sending the energy of your kindness outside of yourself.

A *compliment* is a friendly observation about a person that you say out loud to that person. Giving compliments is a skill that you can use to increase your comfort in social situations, to make friends, and to build relationships. The next exercise will guide you in how to give great compliments.

Exercise 14.3: Giving Compliments

Practice noticing things that you admire or things that you like about people in your daily life. We recommend that you start by observing things about people you already know and like, such as friends, family members, or favorite teachers, to give you some practice before you begin thinking about how to compliment someone you don't know very well.

Think of how you can phrase a specific compliment about something that you like or admire about someone you observed. The best compliments are those that aren't too general. For example, you could notice something that you like about someone's clothing, or you could notice the good job someone did on a project. Following are some examples:

- "Brayden, I really like your idea to build a model race car. I've always wanted to do that."
- "Charles, I like your new backpack. You've got tons of different pockets for storing things."
- "Emma, I really like the purple and blue lines that you painted in the poster graphics. The lines totally pop."

A good compliment needs to be genuine. In other words, when you give a compliment, you should really mean what you say so that the other person believes you and feels as if he or she can trust you. So be sure to make the compliment about something that you really do like or admire about the other person. You don't have to think that something is the best thing in the world, but you should like it at least a little bit so that you can be sincere when you give your compliment.

Try taking a moment right now to think about people you observed today—people you feel most comfortable with—whom you could give compliments to. Be prepared to give some compliments tomorrow.

When you have a specific compliment in mind to give to someone, first notice what he or she is doing. For example, if the person you have chosen to give a compliment to is busy talking to someone else, don't go right up to her, because she might want to be left alone to continue her conversation. Save your compliment for another time, when you and the other person can focus better on each other even for just a moment. It is usually best to say something friendly, such as a compliment, to someone when you are already doing something with him, such as working on a lab project or standing in line.

Don't just walk up to a group of people who are laughing and talking together in a tight circle and start giving compliments, because you might be ignored, or you might be seen as butting in. If you see the person you would like to compliment sitting by herself, however, it might be a good time to try it out.

After you give a compliment, just pause and wait. You need to allow the person to respond. Listening to how a person reacts to your compliment is an important part of the kindness of giving it. A compliment is a kind of gift. When you give a gift to someone, finding out how he feels about the gift is another way to show that you care.

Most of the time, when you give a compliment to someone, you will see a smile or a nod or hear a "thank you." And that can make you feel good too! This doesn't automatically make you best friends if you weren't already, but this is how giving compliments can make it easier to begin to make friends.

Sometimes, when you give a compliment, the other person may feel a little shy and won't respond very much. You can still feel good about giving the compliment, because you reached out and shared kindness with another person.

The more you practice these skills of kindness, the easier it will be to use them. Here is a reminder list of the skills to practice from this chapter:

- Thinking positive wishes for yourself

- Sending kind wishes to others in your mind
- Thinking about and observing others to come up with specific friendly compliments that you might give them
- Saying compliments out loud to others

The more you practice, the easier it will be, and the more kindness you are likely to feel when you are around other people.

Remember:

- You can practice kindness toward yourself by sending yourself good wishes in your thoughts. Practice telling yourself what kind of person you want to be.
- Just thinking about and noticing positive things about people you might want to get to know will make you feel more connected with them. Practice sending good wishes to others in your mind.
- Thinking about and noticing positive things about people you might want to have as friends will help you feel more comfortable when you reach out to those people.
- Look for people who are similar to you and have similar interests. Don't try to make friends with the most popular people in your class if you don't share their interests. Once you have some success with

people who are most like yourself, then you can try this with new people, if you want to.

- Practice coming up with compliments that you could give to different people.
- When you give compliments to others, you are acting like a friend. You might even feel friendlier. People will see you differently and be more interested in getting to know you as a friend. Practice giving genuine compliments to others, starting with people you are already close to.

Practicing kindness involves using your imagination. Try the next exercise just for fun, to stretch your imagination.

Exercise 14.4: Imagine Kindness—Change Your Brain

In the morning when you wake up, imagine the kindest thing you could do for yourself today. Then, imagine the kindest thing you could do for someone else. You can even try to imagine the kindest thing you could do for animals, and then the kindest thing you could do for the planet. Have fun imagining all sorts of things, even if you can't actually do everything you think up.

Recent brain research shows that the more you actively practice kindness toward others, the easier it is to feel friendly toward others. The part of your brain that you use when you practice kindness will begin to grow stronger. The more you exercise kindness through your actions toward others, the more your brain develops the habit of connecting with others. This makes it easier for you to be kind and connect to others in a friendly way. As you direct your life using kindness, you will become better at making friends.

Chapter 15

design your own stage: prepare for your scenes

Both to her family and to kids at school, it seems as if Lily is always in a huff about something. She gets upset over the smallest things. When she gets upset, she becomes totally silent or withdraws from the situation—for example, she goes to her room and locks the door.

When Lily is silent and upset, the people around her usually just ignore her. Her family and her classmates know from experience that she will just get more upset and more withdrawn if they try to do anything to help her. That is because her thinking is shut down. She feels as though she has no options, because she has no idea what she can do to try to make things better. Her only thoughts are of how she feels bad.

Lily could help make things go more smoothly for herself if she were prepared to think about what actions she could take when she gets upset.

In this book, you have learned and practiced many tools for using your body, your mind, and your imagination to take action. You are ready and prepared to take what you have learned in this book into your daily life.

In this chapter, you will think about your life as a kind of stage that you design, where you get to play out the scenes that matter to you. To make changes in your daily life so that you feel less stress and more freedom and independence, you can practice choosing and taking positive action.

Exercise 15.1: Prepare Yourself

You can prepare yourself for the scenes that you will be living through taking positive action. Here are some very simple examples of actions you could take to make your daily life go more smoothly. Maybe you already do some of these things every day as a way of being prepared.

- Before you go to bed at night, if you have school the next day, gather everything you will need to take to school, so that you are prepared.
- Be less reliant on your parents by doing things such as setting your own alarm clock to help you wake up in the morning. If you tend to oversleep, set more than one alarm at different places in your room.

- Make sure that there is always enough of the kind of food you like in your house. If your family uses a shopping list, add the foods that you like to that list. If your family doesn't have a list, you can make a list of your own and give it to the person in your family who usually does the grocery shopping. You could even offer to do the grocery shopping so that you can buy the foods that you like.

- Be ready to prepare your own breakfast in the morning and your own snack after school. You will feel more independent when you are able to do these things by yourself instead of asking others to do them for you.

- Learn to wash, dry, and put away your own clothes. If you have a washing machine at home, ask an adult to show you how to use it. If your family washes clothes at a Laundromat, ask an adult to show you how to use the machines there. This way, you can always have the clothes that you want to wear clean and ready to go.

- Ask a parent or other family member how you can earn money by doing chores around the house. Doing a household chore is a way of giving kindness to others, being part of a family team, and making money at the same time!

Can you think of any other actions to add to this list?

When you imagine all the scenes in your day and think about how you want each scene to end, you will find there are things you can do to help your scenes go the way you want them to.

Thinking about how a scene will end means thinking about goals that you have and the outcomes that you want. The following exercise will show you a way to do that.

Exercise 15.2: Plan for Good Outcomes

Part 1. Think about an upcoming scene in your daily life, such as coming home after school tomorrow. Clearly imagine the way you would like that scene to play out. For example, maybe you want to come home, have a snack, and just relax on the couch. Now, think about how you can make that happen. In other words, what needs to be in place in that scene to produce the outcome that you want? What steps or positive actions can you take to make sure everything goes right with your plan?

In the example of wanting to relax with a snack, a positive action you could take is to let your family members know before you leave for school that you just want to relax with a snack after school, so that they don't ask you to do something as soon as you get home. Another positive action you could take is to be sure that the snack food that you want is already in the house.

Then, the most important part of daily living in any scene is to ***be flexible***! Know and accept the fact that scenes change all the time. No matter how well you have designed the stage and set the scene with a certain outcome in mind, things won't always happen the way you planned. You might need to make changes as the scene plays out.

Be sure to use your breath to stay calm while you do so, so that you are ready to take positive action with each change.

Here is a specific example of designing your own stage and preparing for a scene by thinking about how you want it to end.

You want to have your morning scene go well, with as little stress as possible before you go to school. You imagine everything that needs to happen in order for the scene to go as you would like it to. Then, you think about all the different ways you can prepare for that scene so that things have a good chance of going according to your "creative vision":

- You can decide to go to bed by 11:00 p.m. so that when you wake up at 7:00 a.m., you will feel well rested. Feeling well rested will help you be in a better mood in the morning, not be tired, and remember everything you need to remember.

- You can set an alarm for 10:30 at night, to help you remember to start getting ready for bed at about this time. That way, if you become so engrossed in a video game or TV show that you forget about the time, you will have an alarm reminder. A half hour should give you enough time to prepare for the morning and get yourself ready for bed.

- You can set your alarm for 7:00 a.m., to help you wake up on time without one of your parents yelling at you. This will help reduce everyone's stress.

- You can pack your backpack for school before you go to bed. When everything that you need—your books, homework, pens, paper—is in your backpack, in the morning, all you will have to do is grab it and go!

- You can think about what you would like to eat for breakfast and check to be sure it is in the house.

If you discover that your favorite breakfast food isn't in the house, remember to ***be flexible***! Take one or two deep, calming breaths and just choose a different food. You still have choice. This is an example of taking positive action to make changes to your scene while you are living it. For example, if you are out of toaster pastries, decide to have toast with jam. Practicing flexibility while staying calm will make you feel like a winner! You can put toaster pastries on the shopping list or ask whether someone can get them for you the next time he or she goes to the store.

Part 2. Return to the scene you imagined at the beginning of part 1 and think again of how you would like it to go. Try to clearly imagine the good outcome. Then, ask yourself, what actions do you need to take to prepare yourself for the scene? What actions do you need to take to design the stage? How can you prepare yourself to ***be flexible*** when some part of the scene needs to change? Do these things, and then see the positive effects they can have on your scene and your whole day.

Sometimes, you won't be able to make all the changes you want. In those cases, the most powerful thing that you can do is decide to accept things as they are. Simply accepting what's going on, even if you don't particularly like it, is a positive action. You can then use your energy to focus on what you can actually change.

Being in charge of designing your own stage and creating your own scenes is a great use of your imagination. You can enjoy creating and designing while you build your independence. You will be directing your own life.

Chapter 16

live your own scripts: direct your next steps

Sean often feels frustrated about many things in his life. He spends most of his time and energy reacting to or rebelling against people, rules, and situations he doesn't like in an effort to change his life, but this just leads to more stress.

For example, if his parents want him to do his homework when he gets home from school, Sean gets frustrated, because that is when he wants to chill out and watch TV. Then he gets angry. The anger stresses him out, and then he yells at his parents, "I'm going to watch TV, and you can't stop me." This results in his parents taking TV away from him for the rest of the week. He ends up with a worse outcome than before. Instead of getting what he wants, he loses what he wants.

Taking action is different from reacting. As a teenager, you might find that you are often reacting by rebelling. What does rebelling look like? Rebelling looks like doing the opposite of what someone wants you to do. The trouble with rebelling is that it isn't really an independent action. When you are rebelling, you are stuck in a reaction, instead of being free to make your own choice of action. When you are upset or angry at what is happening around you, you might notice that you start to rebel. This is normal during the teenage years, because this is the time in people's lives when they want to learn to be independent, and teenagers sometimes confuse the idea of independence with rebellion. It is important that you know the distinction. Independence is about making choices and taking positive action. Rebellion involves reacting to things and people in ways that make you feel frustrated and stuck.

In your life, you need to interact with other people to get what you want. You may have to ask for help, negotiate, discuss, and most importantly, listen to others.

There will be many times when you might not be successful in getting what you want. There will be times when it might be hard for you to tell people what you want or need. At these times, you may feel frustrated and rebel against doing anything. Rebellion can lead to feeling shut down with no way to take action.

Sometimes the things you feel like rebelling against are actually things that could help you feel more independent and in charge of your own life. This chapter is about how you can change the script you are living so that instead of getting stuck in rebellion, you can gain more independence. Then, you will be directing your life in a positive, active way.

Exercise 16.1: Five Questions to Help You Write Your Own Script

Take a moment right now to think of some specific things you could ask to do, and put these thoughts into sentences. For example:

- I want to design a new kind of fish tank.
- I want to take a course in animation.
- I would like to watch this magic show.
- I would like to go to drama camp this summer.
- I want to earn money walking dogs in my neighborhood after school.

To make any of these things happen, first, ask yourself the following five specific questions:

1. ***Who is the right person for me to discuss my ideas with?*** For example, if you want to design a new kind of fish tank, think about talking to your uncle who is a marine biologist.
2. ***What information do I need to give to other people so that they will understand what I want to do and why I want to do it?*** For example, if you want to go to drama camp, think about telling your family about your desire to try acting.
3. ***How can I imagine different outcomes?*** For example, imagine writing a story about yourself and what you want,

with several different endings. Then, choose the ending that suits you the best.

4. ***How can I be flexible and listen to suggestions from other people?*** Remember that you are in charge of whom you choose to ask for suggestions, and you are in charge of choosing which, if any, of that person's ideas to follow. This way, you can be free to listen.

5. ***How can I stay positive, confident, and curious while I ask for what I want?*** Breathe deeply, then sit or stand in a confident posture. Breathe again, then use a clear, calm voice to ask for what you want. When you get a response, just breathe, while you plan your next action in your mind.

You will now be more likely to get what you want, because you can write your own script. Just as in a play, your "script" is what you will say out loud. In this case, you will be speaking clearly about what you want (also known as advocating for yourself, which you learned about in chapter 12). In order to do this, you need to believe in your own ideas, be able to speak them clearly, and listen carefully to others' responses.

Here is an example of how writing your own script can help you advocate for yourself. Let's say you are interested in acting. One day, you hear about a drama camp that you want to go to. You start to get upset because your negative thoughts say that your mother will never allow you to go. But then you pause and remember the five questions. You say to yourself: "Wait a minute. I am going to review the five questions so that I can take positive action to get what I want." Then, you review the five questions and make a plan. You research the drama camp online so that you have the facts that would help you convince your mother to let you go. Then, you figure out the best time to talk with your mother (such as when she isn't tired). Then, you make your proposal and stay open to listen to her response so that you can stay in the conversation without closing down your mind with negative thoughts and without letting your anger cause a meltdown if things don't go the way you hoped (remember to pause and breathe deeply).

What if you don't get what you want the first time that you ask? Don't react with anger. Use your pause button. Stay calm and walk away, to give yourself time to make a new plan.

If you suddenly get a great idea, and feel very excited, but not yet clear about what you want, pause and say something like this silently to yourself: "Wait a minute—this is so exciting I can't think straight! I have to write this down so I can figure out what to do. I have to talk about this with my parents. I need to get answers to the five questions!"

When you decide to live your own script, you are choosing to be independent and active instead of being rebellious or withdrawn. You will be able to choose to negotiate to get what you want or what you need by speaking up for yourself, describing your strengths and challenges.

We recommend thinking of your challenges as opportunities for learning and living a good life. When you learn something new, it is always a little scary and exciting at the same time, simply because you don't know everything about what you might have to do. It is like being at the edge of the unknown, and the unknown makes everyone a little nervous.

Exploring means taking risks. So, invite yourself to learn and grow with your challenges. All of us are busy learning and growing all the time, whether we are doing things that are easy or hard. Whenever you feel frustrated when you try to do something you are really interested in, there are things you can say to yourself that will help you be curious and stay calm.

Exercise 16.2: Positive Self-Talk

Here are some examples of things you can say to help you deal with challenging and frustrating situations in a positive, curious way:

- "This is something that I am learning about."
- "This is surprising—I wonder what I can do or say next that will help me learn more."
- "This is a new situation for me, and I am curious to learn from it."

What else could you say to yourself as a reminder that you, like everyone else, are an active, curious human being?

When you make the choice to live your own scripts and direct your next steps, you will be figuring out how to get what you want without reacting or rebelling. When you feel frustrated, you can practice facing situations with real curiosity instead. You will be taking responsibility for yourself by being honest about what would be helpful to you as a student, as a friend, as an artist, as a musician, as a gamer, or as anything else. You will be living your own scripts and directing your own life by including other people as you go about living the kind of life you want.

In directing your next steps, keep these big personal questions in mind:

- What kind of life do you want to live?
- What kinds of work do you like doing? What kinds of jobs involve that kind of work?

Dare to imagine. Dare to dream.

We encourage you to practice the skills you have learned in this book as much as you can in your everyday life. With practice, you can direct your next steps every day in a calm, confident way. Through practice, you will be choosing to build your independence and your connection with other people. The more you can direct your own life, the more fun you will have just being yourself.

We welcome your ideas. We welcome your flexibility, curiosity, and playfulness. We welcome you!

Irene McHenry, PhD, is a licensed psychologist, dynamic educator, consultant, and the author and editor of numerous publications, including *Tuning In: Mindfulness in Teaching and Learning*. She leads programs nationwide with a focus on leadership and mindfulness. McHenry was founding head of Delaware Valley Friends School (for teens with learning differences), cofounder of Greenwood Friends School, founding faculty for Fielding Graduate University's doctoral program in education, and a senior investigator for the Mind and Life Summer Research Institute. She directs the Leadership Institute and mindfulness programs for Friends Council on Education where she recently served as executive director. She is past-president for the Council for American Private Education and serves on the boards of Mindfulness in Education Network, Vector Group Consulting North America, and Haverford College.

Carol Moog, PhD, founder of ImagineAct, recently served as the clinical director of the Social Learning Disorders Program at the University of Pennsylvania. She is the psychologist at The Miquon School, actively collaborates with Autism Inclusion Resources (AIR), and works extensively with children, teens, and adults on the autism spectrum in her clinical practice as a licensed psychologist. Carol was an artist-in-residence at Green Tree School and a consultant to the Social Competency Program at the Center for Autism, creating theater-based social skills programs for teens drawing from her experience as a theater improviser, actor, musician, communications consultant, and writer. Among her publications, she is the author of *Are They Selling Her Lips? Advertising and Identity*. Carol has been interviewed by the *Wall Street Journal*, the *New York Times*, *Newsweek*, the *Philadelphia Inquirer*, *USA Today*, National Public Radio's *Fresh Air*, the *Today Show*, and *Good Morning America*.

Foreword writer **Susan Kaiser Greenland, JD,** is a former corporate attorney who developed the Inner Kids mindful awareness program for children, teens, and families. Research on the Inner Kids elementary school program was conducted at the Mindful Awareness Research Center at UCLA and is published in the *Journal of Applied School Psychology.* Author of *The Mindful Child,* Susan teaches children, parents, and professionals and consults with various organizations on teaching mindful awareness in an age-appropriate and secular manner. She has spoken at universities, medical centers, and schools, both public and private, worldwide. Susan lives in Los Angeles with her husband Seth Greenland. They have two grown children.

MORE BOOKS *from* NEW HARBINGER PUBLICATIONS

THE SHYNESS & SOCIAL ANXIETY WORKBOOK FOR TEENS

CBT and ACT Skills to Help You Build Social Confidence

ISBN: 978-1608821877 / US $16.95

Also available as an e-book

Instant Help Books
An Imprint of New Harbinger Publications

THE SOCIAL SUCCESS WORKBOOK FOR TEENS

Skill-Building Activities for Teens with Nonverbal Learning Disorder, Asperger's Disorder & Other Social-Skill Problems

ISBN: 978-1572246140 / US $14.95

Also available as an e-book

Instant Help Books
An Imprint of New Harbinger Publications

THE ANXIETY WORKBOOK FOR TEENS

Activities to Help You Deal with Anxiety & Worry

ISBN: 978-1572246034 / US $14.95

Also available as an e-book

Instant Help Books
An Imprint of New Harbinger Publications

HELPING YOUR CHILD WITH AUTISM SPECTRUM DISORDER

A Step-by-Step Workbook for Families

ISBN: 978-1572243842 / US $27.95

Also available as an e-book

THE STRESS REDUCTION WORKBOOK FOR TEENS

Mindfulness Skills to Help You Deal with Stress

ISBN: 978-1572246973 / US $15.95

Also available as an e-book

Instant Help Books
An Imprint of New Harbinger Publications

THE EXECUTIVE FUNCTIONING WORKBOOK FOR TEENS

Help for Unprepared, Late & Scattered Teens

ISBN: 978-1608826568 / US $16.95

Also available as an e-book

Instant Help Books
An Imprint of New Harbinger Publications

new**harbinger**publications
1-800-748-6273 / newharbinger.com

(VISA, MC, AMEX / prices subject to change without notice)

 Like us on Facebook  Follow us on Twitter @newharbinger.com

Don't miss out on new books in the subjects that interest you.
Sign up for our **Book Alerts** at **newharbinger.com/bookalerts**